If You Want Success, Be Happy!

-4 Simple Steps To Have It All Without Sacrificing Yourself

Second edition

Written by Majbrit Bøttger

www.majbrit.coach

Dedication

I want to dedicate this book to Carsten, the love of my life, who always stand by me and tirelessly supports me through all and any of my projects with all his heart, soul, and wisdom - thank you!

And to my three beautiful daughters Emma, Freja and Klara for their endless love and support. What a gift and a blessing to be your mother.

Many people helped shape me along the way. Still, some directly impacted me and taught me valuable life lessons I have carried with me ever since. One of those people is Tanja Olsen, who you will meet in this book. Tanja has always, along with Pia Bram Jørgensen, been my rock. The kind of friends I can call in the middle of the night (and I have), and they will jump in the car, drive across the country, and not even ask why. Thank you for being in my life; I love you.

Next on this list is a man who had made a tremendous impact on my life and made a huge difference exactly when I needed it the most, Brendon Burchard. When I met him, I was a hot mess, but he snapped me out of it by making me take action, and he has been an inspiration and a mentor ever since. So much of what I teach others today I have learned from Brendon, and he will always be my hero.

Dean Graziosi, Wesley Virgin, Ted McGrath, and Raimonda Jan have also been great influencers to me and taught me so much about mindset, business, and life. I owe them all a big thanks for their knowledge, insights, and authentic desire to help others. I wouldn't be here if it weren't for you.

Many other people have inspired, challenged, and believed in me throughout this journey. I appreciate all of you for that.

As you read this book, I sincerely hope you can feel the heartfelt wishes for your success from the people who are the reason this book exists, and me.

Table of Content

Welcome

Love Yourself First

You are the most important person in your life and need to love, nourish, and care for yourself. Let this be the first lesson in this book. If you don't adopt this mindset, you are at great risk of burning out, and you will not be able to be all you want for others. But you are here. You decided to change something in your life and took action. That puts you right into the top 2% in this world. Celebrate that!

Most people complain about their life or situation but will not take any action to change what they don't like. But you are here, and I have put my heart and soul into this book to provide you with the knowledge and strategies you need to make the changes necessary to reach your goals and dreams.

I'm honored that you have put your trust in me to be the one to help you get where you want to go. It will likely not be easy, but I guarantee it will be worth the effort, and I will be here the whole time to guide you, support you, and break it down for you, so you don't get overwhelmed.

I'm excited to share everything with you here.

- Majbrit

How to Read This Book

I've made my fair share of mistakes and am still here to tell the tale. Yes, this is a personal development book, but it's really about designing a better life for yourself and those you love. An everyday life that brings you joy, energy, rewards, and even peace in both life and career. Learning from my mistakes and use the tools provided in this book will help you get there faster.

Do you feel like you're just going through the motions in life? Do you want to break free from the limitations holding you back and create a life that truly fulfills you? Then this book is for you.

So, welcome to a journey of self-discovery and positive change! Through more than a decade of research, trial, and error, I have distilled proven strategies for creating a clear vision, optimizing your health, taking back command of your life, and fueling your resilience to life's challenges. These are not just theoretical concepts; they have been tested and refined by all my clients who have achieved extraordinary success in their own lives.

I understand that making significant changes in your life can feel overwhelming. That's why I have broken down each strategy into simple, actionable steps you can take at your own pace.

What You'll Learn

1. Creating Your Vision: You will learn how to create your vision and map out the steps to achieve it.

2. Optimizing Your Health: You will optimize your health and energy levels to be at your best daily.

3. Taking Back Command of Your Life: You will take back command of your life and become the master of your destiny.

4. Fueling Your Resilience: You will fuel your resilience to setbacks and challenges so that you can persevere through any obstacle.

Sustainable Change

The approach is not about quick fixes or shortcuts; it's about creating sustainable change that will serve you for the rest of your life. You will learn how to cultivate a growth mindset, embrace your strengths and weaknesses, and develop mastery at overcoming any obstacle that comes your way. And they will come!

Getting Started

You might think, "This all sounds great, but how do I begin?" Don't worry - this book is designed to guide you through each step of the process with practical tips and exercises to help you apply these strategies to your own life. You don't need to have it all figured out or have all the answers right now. The important thing is to take the first step and trust the process.

Unlock Your Full Potential

So, if you're ready to unlock your full potential and achieve your desired life, let's get started. This book will equip you with the tools, knowledge, and mindset you need to succeed. And who knows - this might be the beginning of your most incredible journey yet.

Ready for More?

If you read this book and decide you'd like help implementing its strategies as quickly as possible, please book a call to chat at **www.majbrit.coach/call**. Helping people like you to design the life of their dreams is exactly what I do day in and day out, and I'm here if you need me. Now, let's go!

Part 1

The Foundation

Chapter 1

"The truth does not change according to your Ability to stomach it."

– Flannery O'Connor

Who This Book Is For

At one point, I felt like my life was running me, rather than me running my life. It was a nightmare. I was overwhelmed with sadness, frustration, and loneliness. My short fuse with my kids led to constant guilt, and I felt completely out of control, hopeless, and stupid. I was relentlessly tough on myself.

This brings us to our first important lesson: Your current life is a result of your previous decisions, whether you made them consciously or unconsciously, through action or reaction, with or without guidance. The people surrounding you are the people you designed your life to attract. Your income, the quality of your relationships, your everyday energy and joy, your ability to handle situations, and your pace of getting things done are all consequences of the design you created.

From the outside looking in, I was living the "perfect life." I was married to a man the rest of the world adored; he was charming and helpful. I had a lovely house in a nice town, three beautiful, well-functioning daughters, and a well-paid job. But what I didn't have was the feeling of aliveness.

The worst part is that I adapted. The stress and toxic environment became my new normal. I told myself that I was the problem; I was being difficult and too demanding. This is the path to mental and emotional self-destruction. I was so out of alignment with my core values and my inner integrity that not only did I no longer recognize myself, but I also didn't like who I was becoming and how that felt.

The self-sacrificing hustle has no rewards. Fortunately, I found help before I completely lost myself, leading to the development of a system that has helped people worldwide live the lives they want and deserve.

I was able to reclaim my sanity, my positivity, my joy, and my love for life. I began to sparkle and shine again, making a difference in the world by helping others through their struggles, all due to the changes I'll teach you about in these pages. I changed how I look at myself and how I choose to show up in this world.

There were two specific improvements I made:

1. I took back command of my life, meaning I stopped living based on other people's (assumed) expectations and started living according to my values, feelings, wants, and desires.

2. I designed my life to attract people who support me, my dreams, and my visions, as opposed to those who want to keep me "in check" because they feel more comfortable when things stay the same.

In this book, I will teach you how to take the first steps toward being the leader of your own life.

The first thing you should do right now is head over to: **www.majbrit.coach/book-resources** and download the worksheets. Don't work on them just yet, but have them ready as we move through this book so you can do them along the way. The mind will tell you that you can do it afterward, but we both know that it will never happen. You will miss out on essential reflections, and you won't get the results you could have. Apply the same dedication to the exercises as you have by opening this book. They are designed to help you!

"You have a clean slate every day you wake up. You have a chance every single morning to make that change and be the person you want to be. You just have to decide to do it. Decide today's the day.

Say it: this is going to be my day."

– Brendon Burchard

Embracing a New Perspective

Imagine waking up every morning with a sense of purpose, excitement, and clarity. Picture yourself living a life that aligns with your deepest values and aspirations. This is not a distant dream but a tangible reality that you can achieve by following the principles and practices outlined in this book.

I know firsthand how challenging it can be to break free from old patterns and beliefs that no longer serve you. I remember the days when I felt trapped in a cycle of negativity, feeling like a prisoner of my own life. It was a lonely place, filled with self-doubt and fear. But I also know that change is possible because I have lived it.

The journey to reclaiming your life begins with a single step: the decision to change. This decision sets the stage for a transformative process that will empower you to take control of your destiny. It requires courage, commitment, and a willingness to confront the uncomfortable truths about your current situation. But the rewards are immeasurable.

In this book, you will learn how to identify and dismantle the limiting beliefs that hold you back. You will discover strategies to build resilience, cultivate positive habits, and foster meaningful relationships. These lessons are not theoretical concepts but practical tools that you can apply immediately to create lasting change.

The Power of Community

One of the most important aspects of personal growth is the support of a like-minded community. Surrounding yourself with individuals who share your values and aspirations can provide the encouragement and accountability needed to stay on track. This book is not just a guide but an invitation to join a community of people committed to living their best lives.

The teachings in this book is rooted in the belief that true success is not measured by external achievements but by the quality of your inner life. It emphasizes the importance of aligning your actions with your values, cultivating a positive mindset, and nurturing your well-being. By engaging with peers and embracing these principles, you will experience a profound shift in how you perceive and interact with the world. You will gain the confidence to pursue your dreams and the resilience to overcome obstacles. Most importantly, you will develop a deep sense of gratitude and joy that will sustain you through life's challenges.

Taking Action

The information in this book is only as valuable as the action you take. As you read, I encourage you to actively engage with the exercises and reflections provided. These activities are designed to deepen your understanding and help you integrate the lessons into your daily life.

Set aside time each day to work on the exercises, and be honest with yourself about your progress. Remember, this is not about achieving perfection but about making consistent, meaningful changes. Celebrate your successes, no matter how small, and learn from your setbacks. Each step forward is a step towards a more fulfilling and empowered life.

A Personal Invitation

I invite you to embark on this journey with an open heart and a curious mind. Allow yourself to dream big and envision the life you truly desire. Believe in your ability to create that life, and trust that you have everything you need within you to make it happen.

As you move through this book, know that you are not alone. I am here to guide, and support you. Together, we will navigate the challenges and celebrate the victories. This is your time to shine, and I am honored to be a part of your journey.

Let's begin this transformational journey together. Download the worksheets, immerse yourself in the lessons, and take the first step towards reclaiming your power and joy. Your best life is waiting for you. This is your moment. This is your time to shine.

You are capable of extraordinary things.

Chapter 2

Think about what you can do now,

Not what you wish you had done before.

-Jay Shetty

Reality Check

As you already know I was a mess, but it wasn't something that just happened; I was slowly falling apart. People kept asking if I was okay, and they all got the same answer: "I'm fine; it's just a phase it will pass." I knew I was under a lot of pressure with a divorce, moving to the other end of the country, a new job, and adjusting to being a single mother. Still, my motto was there's only one way, and that is through! Up to that point in my life, I had never known that not to be true.

BUT...I had also never been in a situation quite as chaotic. In reality, I had no idea how to handle it. One morning, I woke up and realized I had lost my ability to find solutions, and it freaked me out. I felt utterly lost, and my three girls, at 3, 6, and 9, were paying the price for my lack of ability to reach out and ask for help. Three little girls were crying because their mom was miserable, and all they wanted to do was help, but they couldn't.

Something had to change. I had to change, but I also knew I was in no position to do it alone. I was too locked down in my situation. And let's face it, if I knew how to move forward from here, I would have stopped this craziness before it got as far as it did. I needed help. It was a very conscious decision I made when I started to work with one of the best coaches in the world. It was never in the cards that I would be working with him, but I met him at an event, and to me, it was a sign of "now is the time."

He made me realize that the only way to regain control of my life was to generate it myself, and he gave me all the tools I needed. That helped me far beyond what I could ever have imagined, and I decided I wanted to help others, so they don't have to go through what I went through but rather experience the feeling of freedom that comes with living a life of purpose, energy, and joy—every day!

This is the power of coaching!

You now know that I'm no superhuman. I have the same challenges and struggles as everyone else. I just got better over time at dealing with them, so they take less time and energy. It's a strategy we will cover in depth later in the book, and it is vital for you to (re)gain your personal power.

In the past year alone, my team and I have helped more than 200 people get to the next level of personal power and freedom.

You don't need to be a superhuman to benefit and grow from what you are about to learn. We will cover the different ways to get there later in the book

The book you are reading right now is much more than just pages of lifehacks and ideas. I'll give you the same science-backed tools and strategies as I do with my private clients to get them to balance, freedom, inner peace, and personal well-being while performing at their A-game in life and career.

The methods in this book are proven by science to be the ones that get you the furthest the fastest.

Taking Action: The Time is Now

Well, it's time to take action! There are only seven days in a week and "someday" is not one of them. And yet, we keep talking about "someday." Someday, when the children are older, then... Someday, I want to travel to... Someday, when I'm not so busy, we can do...

It's always someday, someday, someday. But someday never comes, the only thing you have is TO-DAY! It's time to stop waiting. Instead, figure out how you want to spend the only day you know you're guaranteed. Have you hugged your loved ones? Have you laughed? Have you heard your favorite music? Have you said, "I love you"? Have you delivered the best version of yourself to others? All around us are reminders of how quickly it can be over. Stop waiting!

When you are ready, it's already too late.

—Majbrit Bøttger

Self-Evaluation Exercise

Before we move on, let's tap into where you are right now. Where do you have your strengths and where do you have gaps that need your focus? Rate yourself on a scale from 1-10, 1 being not at all and 10 being Olympian gold level. Use the schedule on the next page.

Once you've rated yourself for each statement, total your scores and then use the Answer Key to determine your next steps. The goal isn't a complete or perfect rating of every nuance of your life but rather a snapshot of your current level and a good opportunity for overall self-reflection.

So, don't stress about the exact wording of these descriptions. Instead, give your overall impression of how you rate each category based on the last six months of your life. Be honest, but don't use it to hit yourself in the head. You are not supposed to know everything yet. If you did, you wouldn't be reading this book.

I'm here to teach you step by step, so trust the process and just follow along.

Painting a Picture of Success

Imagine waking up each morning with a clear mind, a heart full of purpose, and a spirit ready to tackle the day. Envision yourself not just surviving but thriving, finding joy in the little things and strength in every challenge. This system isn't just about achieving goals; it's about transforming your entire approach to life.

Consider what it would feel like to walk into a room and instantly connect with others, exuding confidence and positivity. Imagine having a toolbox of strategies to handle any situation with grace and ease. Think about the peace of mind that comes from knowing you are living in alignment with your core values and aspirations.

This vision can be your reality. The journey begins with the decision to change and is fueled by the strategies and tools you'll find in this book. You will learn how to break free from limiting beliefs, cultivate a positive mindset, and design a life that attracts support and joy. This isn't a quick fix but a sustainable transformation that empowers you to take control of your destiny.

The Role of a Coach

You might be wondering, why a coach? Think of a coach as your guide through uncharted territories, someone who sees your potential even when you don't. My coach helped me see that the only way to regain control was to take the reins myself. He provided the tools and strategies I needed to rebuild my life from the ground up.

A coach doesn't just give advice; they offer accountability, perspective, and support. They help you uncover the answers within yourself and encourage you to take bold steps forward. The changes I made under my coach's guidance were profound, setting me on a path of continuous growth and fulfillment. Now, I aim to pass on these transformative techniques to you.

Embracing Your Journey

The journey you are about to embark on is unique to you. It's filled with opportunities for growth, challenges that will test your resolve, and moments of profound clarity and joy. Embrace each step, knowing that you are capable of extraordinary change.

As you move forward, remember that every small action you take compounds into significant progress.

Celebrate your wins, learn from your setbacks, and stay committed to your vision. This book is your roadmap, and each chapter is a step towards a more empowered and joyful life.

You are not alone in this journey. The community that surrounds you, the stories you will hear, and the exercises you will complete are all part of a collective effort to inspire and uplift each other. Together, we can achieve more than we ever could alone.

Final Thoughts

This book is more than a collection of strategies; it is an invitation to transform your life. As you engage with the content, take the exercises seriously, and apply the lessons, you will begin to see changes. Not just in your external circumstances, but in your inner world as well.

Your time is now. The decision to change is the first step towards a life filled with purpose, energy, and joy. Trust in the process, believe in yourself, and take action. The journey to your best life starts today.

Let's get started.

Self-Evaluation

Health 1 2 3 4 5 6 7 8 9 10

My overall physical health is optimized to make me feel energetic, motivated and strong each day. I take care of myself so that I can feel my best.

Mindset 1 2 3 4 5 6 7 8 9 10

I can bounce back from challenges and I know how to accept and adapt to make the best of every situation. I can see opportunities and are not afraid of trying new things outside my comfort zone.

Love 1 2 3 4 5 6 7 8 9 10

I feel a consistently deep, mutual, trusting, and loving connection with my significant other. We are patient, respectful an attentive to each other's wants and needs.

Family 1 2 3 4 5 6 7 8 9 10

My immediate circle of family brings connection, fun and positive energy into my life and I do my very best to bring positive energy into all my interactions with them.

Friends 1 2 3 4 5 6 7 8 9 10

I have a strong and meaningful connection with my inner circle of friends. They are supportive of my dreams and visions. They listen to me and challenge me to grow and I do the same for them.

Mission 1 2 3 4 5 6 7 8 9 10

I have a clear mission in my work-life. I love my work and I feel the contribution I make is valuable and meaningful. I strive to be excellent in my efforts every day.

Finances 1 2 3 4 5 6 7 8 9 10

My income supports the lifestyle I desire for myself and my family. I have a clear vision for improving my finances and lifestyle in the next few years.

Free time 1 2 3 4 5 6 7 8 9 10

I spend time, on a consistent basis, on things I love to do outside work and obligations. I have "me-time" scheduled to refuel and recharge.

Spirit 1 2 3 4 5 6 7 8 9 10

I feel a deep connection to myself and the present moment. My values and beliefs are present in all my daily actions and decisions.

Self-love 1 2 3 4 5 6 7 8 9 10

I speak only nice words to myself. I think of myself as being the most important person in my life and I pamper myself so I can recharge.

Answer Key

Score 1-50

The Fundamentals Are Missing.

The bad news is that you must include core, fundamental elements required for long-term success. You probably already know and feel this every day. The good news is that all of that can be fixed, and even better, it means you get to redesign and establish these fundamentals from the ground up. Read this book with curiosity and implement what you learn, and you will be fired up faster than you ever thought possible.

Score 51-75

Consistency Is Key

If your score got you to this section, you have some good habits in play but need more consistency and routine. Consider changing some of your habits for new ones you can stick to more easily. Read this book with curiosity, implement what is relevant for you, and you'll hit the ground running.

Score 76-100

Challenge

You are doing good, and you have a lot of reflection and habits in place. You are actively working on reaching the next level. At some point, it is hard to do that on your own. You can only challenge yourself so much. If the next level of joy, freedom, and performance is your goal, all you have to do is implement what I teach you in this book, and you are on the way to the stars, my friend.

Get the worksheet at

www.majbrit.coach/book-resources

Chapter 3

You can practice shooting eight hours a day, but if your technique is wrong, then all you become is very good at shooting the wrong way. Get the fundamentals down and the level of everything you do will rise.

-Michael Jordan

Four Lessons Learned

For over a decade, I've dedicated myself to studying and coaching individuals from more than 20 different countries, and every imaginable background. Throughout this journey, I've identified four recurring issues that not only plagued those I worked with but also challenged me during the most tumultuous times of my life. These lessons, hard-earned and transformative, are the pillars of my current success and well-being.

Let's take a step back in time. This perspective shift will illuminate these lessons with a clarity that can inspire profound change in your own life.

principles can be applied in your own journey toward personal power and freedom. Embrace these insights, reflect on them deeply, and take the necessary steps to implement them in your life. Your path to empowerment begins with the choices you make today.

#1: Don't Carry Other People's Luggage

Let me start by saying that today, I have a genuinely positive relationship with my ex-husband, the father of my three girls. We collaborate seamlessly when it comes to important events for our daughters, such as graduations and birthdays. We talk like friends, can comfortably share the same space.

However, right after our divorce, the situation was far from amicable. His frustration manifested in angry outbursts, regardless of who was present. His rage and yelling were terrifying for our daughters, who were just three, six, and nine years old at the time. The tension was palpable, and it affected every aspect of our lives.

Eventually, we moved to create a safer environment, but he started calling me instead. His phone calls were filled with screaming, yelling, and relentless berating. He even took me to court twice to seek custody of our eldest daughter, forcing her to be present in court at the tender ages of ten and eleven. This all transpired within eighteen months, leaving me as a nervous wreck. I was perpetually sad, angry, frustrated, and anxious, constantly bracing myself for his next outburst. I felt like I was walking on eggshells, fearing the next storm that would shatter our fragile peace.

At one point, my dear friend Tanja said to me, "Don't you think it's time for him to carry his own luggage?" Initially, I didn't understand what she meant, so she elaborated. "You walk around like the living dead, always on edge, anticipating what might happen next. Your emotions and your mood are harming yourself, your better judgment, your children, and your performance at work. The only person not affected by this is him. Don't let him control your mood and emotions anymore; he doesn't deserve that power over you. Take your power back!"

The next time he lashed out at me, I responded with, "Do what you feel like you have to do," and waited. Although it took a few attempts to do it convincingly, mostly because I had to convince myself first, it worked. I reclaimed my power, and his anger gradually diminished. This marked the beginning of a relationship where we could first communicate about the essentials, then collaborate for our daughters' sake, and eventually talk like friends about our lives. and he has been immensely supportive in building my company to where it is today, so I get to pursuit my mission to make a significant impact in the world.

This advice has proven invaluable countless times since, even in less dramatic situations. Whenever I'm tempted to get angry, I remember Tanja's words: "They don't deserve to have control over your mood and emotions—take your power back!"

Reflect on this:

- Do you have anyone in your life who needs to carry their own luggage?

- What can you say to them to make them understand that you will no longer participate in their drama?

- What can you say to yourself to remind you to keep your power?

#2: Start In The Kitchen

Life can sometimes feel overwhelming, leaving you unsure of what to do next. This brings me to the second life-changing lesson I learned.

After buying a new house, I had to move everything on my own. In three days, I walked 68,742 steps, moving everything from chairs to closets by myself, with the exception of two couches, which I had help with. Once everything was moved, I closed the door and turned around to face 68 extra-large boxes that needed unpacking, while my three little girls looked at me with hungry eyes.

Feeling utterly overwhelmed, I slid down the door and sat on the floor. After about ten minutes, I called Tanja. When she arrived, she assessed the situation and said, "Start in the kitchen, and I'll go buy us dinner.

This experience taught me two crucial lessons. First, have a friend like Tanja—someone who will drop everything and come to your aid without hesitation. Second, don't hesitate to ask for help, and do so sooner than you think you need to. Sometimes, all you need is someone to give you direction and set you in motion, and you can handle it from there

Whenever life feels overwhelming, I remember Tanja's advice: "start in the kitchen." It reminds me to break down tasks into manageable steps, no matter how daunting they seem.

Reflect on this:

- Do you have a friend who would drive four hours to help you without asking any questions?

- How can you cultivate relationships that offer such unwavering support?

- What's one area of your life right now where you can "start in the kitchen" and take the first step to make progress?

#3: Perfect Is Trouble

Perfection is just another word for fear. Read that again: perfection is just another word for fear. Let me share how I discovered this truth.

When I started my business, I wanted everything to be flawless. I immersed myself in continuous education—more courses, more certifications, more knowledge. Every time someone suggested it was time to take action, I'd reply, "I just need to learn a bit more about creating videos, mastering content, or building a website." For two years, I was stuck in this cycle, convinced I needed to be perfectly prepared before I could begin. Although the knowledge I gained was valuable, I could have started much sooner if I had only mustered the courage.

Reflecting on when I had my first child, I remember walking into a store filled with baby equipment. They convinced me to buy everything, claiming it was all essential for my precious little one. As it turned out, I didn't use half of it. By the time my second child arrived, I used even less. Why do we believe we need to be perfect to start?

I compare this to learning how to ride a bike. When I was a kid, we didn't have training wheels. My dad would use a broomstick to hold the bicycle upright and run beside me. Once he felt I had the balance, he would let go, and I would inevitably fall. We repeated this process until I finally got it right. As a child, I accepted falls and bruises as part of the learning journey. I didn't expect to ride perfectly the first time I got on a bike.

When it came to shooting my first video course, I was incredibly nervous. My palms were sweaty, even though I was alone in my kitchen. It finally dawned on me that if I didn't like the video, I could simply delete it and start over. I did those modules countless times, striving for a perfect one-take. But in the end, nobody cared about the minor flaws.

I realized I'd been afraid for no reason.

The feedback I received was overwhelmingly positive. People loved the course and how it transformed their lives. Not a single person commented on the lighting, the one-take execution, or the sound quality. Years later, I watch those early videos and see their imperfections. Yet, the videos I create now are still mostly one-takes. I don't redo them just because I stumble over a word or say something silly. Enthusiasm and authenticity always trump polish.

If there's something you've been holding back on, get started. It's all about taking action. I didn't know how to build a business. I feared making mistakes, scaring away customers, and messing up. So, I did nothing and hid behind the illusion of perfection. But let me tell you this: perfect is an illusion. What's perfect to me might not be perfect to you.

You will never know what perfect means to someone else, so you will always fall short. Don't set yourself up for that kind of failure. Strive for excellence and do your best.

As long as you can go to bed at night and say, "I did great today; I'm proud of what I accomplished, how I behaved, and how I treated others," then you're as close to perfect as you'll ever need to be. But you still need to start.

Reflect on this:

- Where do you need to let go of your perfectionism?

- How can you do it differently?

- What positive feeling can you generate from this?

#4: Success Comes From Happiness

I used to believe that happiness was a reward for achieving success. I thought that once I got a new job, a raise, built a successful business, or met the man of my dreams, I would be happy. I placed all my faith in external circumstances—things I couldn't fully control. But the truth is, happiness doesn't come from success; success comes from happiness.

Happiness is a state of mind rather than a destination. Once I realized this, everything began to change. Deciding to be happy required me to adopt a new perspective on life and develop habits that supported this mindset. I started paying closer attention to where I directed my thoughts and mental energy.

You see, you get what you focus on.

If you constantly think about the bad economy, crises, problems, and worries, you will gradually lose hope for your future. If you stop believing in a better way and settle for the status quo, you will get stuck in mediocrity or, worse, fall into a funk that saps your initiative. The scary part is, you might not even notice; you simply adapt.

Conversely, if you consciously choose to focus on what you have, what you can do, and what you want, you create a solid foundation for success. This shift will leave you feeling empowered and motivated to pursue your dreams and goals.

Later in the book, I will delve deeper into how you can change your mindset for success, and you'll find game-changing exercises to help you implement these changes.

Reflect on this:

- What should you stop worrying about?

- What should you start focusing on right now?

- What positive difference will it make for others if you change your focus?

- What positive difference will it make for yourself if you change your focus?

These lessons form the cornerstone of personal growth and success. By letting go of the illusion of perfection and embracing happiness as a state of mind, you set yourself on a path to true fulfillment and achievement. The journey might be challenging, but the rewards are immeasurable. As you continue reading, keep these principles in mind, and let them guide you toward a life filled with purpose, joy, and success.

Chapter 4

"Change will not come if we wait for some other person or some other time. We are the ones we've been waiting for. We are the change that we seek."

-Barack Obama

Challenge of Change

Our current belief system and surroundings challenge us whenever we want to make changes. We will meet resistance and can easily be trapped in a negative spiral, quitting before we even start. To better understand what might be holding you back, let's explore what I believe to be the most common factors that stop people in their tracks.

Whenever you want to make a change in your life, you will also have to deal with resistance from several fronts. Your brain is lazy and will not accept changes on your first try, so you must be very structured. I will teach you how in this book. You start with creating a routine; if you repeat it enough, it will become a habit, and over time that habit will become a part of your DNA.

External Resistance

You will also likely have to deal with resistance from people around you. Most people live within their comfort zone, and by making changes to your life, you will rattle their sense of comfort. They will try to pull you back to where they feel comfortable. This resistance can manifest in various ways, often as seemingly well-intentioned warnings like, "Are you sure?", "Is this a good idea?", "Have you thought it through?", or the dreaded "what ifs" and "you're too..." followed by a negative statement.

These comments might come from a place of concern, but they can quickly make you doubt yourself and your mission. Be mindful of whom you pay attention to. A golden rule is, don't listen to anyone who hasn't done what you want to do. If you want to start a business, only listen to people running successful businesses. Those who have tried and failed, or worse, never tried but only heard about someone who failed, will tell you it's impossible because they couldn't do it. Don't lower your standards and commitment to other people's convictions. You are better than that!

Building a Strong Foundation

You might be thinking, "Hey, I didn't get this book for you to tell me what I'm doing wrong," and I get it. But hang in there, and you will soon find out why this is an essential part of your path to growth and success. It's like building a house. If you do it on an unstable foundation, it will collapse, so you need to replace that foundation with a new and stronger one if you want your house to be safe and solid for years to come.

The same goes for your personal growth and development. You don't want to build good habits on top of bad ones. So instead, replace them and leave the fixer-upper solutions to the politicians.

Clarity

Not being crystal clear on what you want will create two problems. First, you will only reach your destination if you know what it is. You will dabble around if you don't know what you want, leaving your life to chance and coincidence. If you don't know why you want it, you will be half-committed. You kind of want it, but you kind of don't, and you will kind of work on it—sometimes! You have to level up your ambition; otherwise, you can never improve your performance because you won't care enough. Own your ambition, and come hell or high water, stick with it, or you will end up lowering your dreams to fit other people's mediocrity. The fact that you are here reading this book tells me you don't want to settle for that.

The first step is to define your goals and dreams clearly. To move forward, you first need to know precisely what you want to accomplish. This might seem obvious, but many people don't pay enough attention to this part of the process.

Surprisingly, many people don't know what they want, but you can bet they know what they don't want, and more often than not, that is how people respond when I ask them what they want in life.

"I don't want to stay in this job, that's for sure." "I don't want a relationship like my last one." "I don't want to worry about my finances constantly;" you get the picture!

Imagine you called the local pizza place and said, "I'd like to order a pizza; I don't want pineapple." You would never reach the finish line, and on top, the pizza guy would have to make guesses between all the things you didn't mention, and chances are that you would end up with a pizza you don't like. The same thing goes for life. Put in an order for what you want and be crystal clear about it.

The Two Sides of Clarity

Your clarity has two sides to it. One is your goal, and the other is your purpose. Many people can, by being thoughtful, dial in on their goal because it is measurable and often tangible.

The second step is to find your purpose, your meaningfulness, your why, or however you prefer to describe it. Most find the word "purpose" too divine or too big. Don't worry; it is just another word for whatever brings you meaningfulness and satisfaction in your life.

Your purpose is strongly tied to your core values and inner integrity, meaning things you feel are right and something you would do regardless of prestige, money, or fame, but solely because it made you feel good.

You should start here. I have seen countless examples of people having a goal and never reaching it. When we dive into the reason, they find that their goal is based on what they believe they should be doing based on other people's expectations, education, history, financial situation, or whatever the case. The one missing thing was the alignment with their values and inner integrity. Whatever the goal was, it didn't make them happy and fulfilled.

If you start with the purpose, you will have a far better chance of succeeding in reaching your goals.

Your purpose or "why" needs to be strong enough for you to push through when things get tough. Your "why" is your anchor.

You will have to dive deeply into your soul to answer this. Seven layers deep, to be exact. Not five, not nine—seven. That is the number of "why's" you need to ask yourself to go from your head (rational thinking) to your heart (emotional meaningfulness). We will get into this exercise I learned from Dean Graziosi (who was taught by Dan Sullivan) later in the book. Just keep in mind that your initial thought about it might not be correct.

Embrace the Change

Change is never easy, and the resistance you face is a natural part of the process. But remember, you are not alone. Everyone who has ever achieved something significant has faced resistance and had to push through it. By understanding the sources of resistance and developing strategies to overcome them, you are laying the groundwork for lasting success.

As you continue reading, keep these principles in mind. They will serve as your guide, helping you navigate the challenges and stay focused on your goals. Embrace the journey with an open heart and a determined spirit. You have the power to create the life you desire, and this book will provide you with the tools and insights to make it happen.

Reflect on these questions:

- *What resistance have you faced in the past when trying to make changes?*

- *How can you better prepare yourself to overcome this resistance in the future?*

- *Who in your life supports your growth, and how can you lean on them more?*

Your path to personal growth and success is just beginning. With clarity, purpose, and the right mindset, you can achieve anything you set your mind to.

Courage

Change and action take courage. We often set our minds to something and are dedicated to it until it's time to take action. I did that when I started my business, remember? I had all the skills I needed to make a difference in people's lives and make an impact, and I was all fired up about the chance to help others and save them time and frustration by sharing my own story and experiences.

But then, I froze. Instead of taking action, I buried myself in more education and more knowledge. Knowledge is great, but it carries no value if you don't use it to take action. One of my coaches pointed this out to me in a very tough-love way, and I committed to doing my first video before our next session two weeks later. He convinced me that I had everything I needed to jump on camera and speak. I was ready to finally make a difference.

With help, I set up a "studio" in my kitchen. I spent the better part of a day setting the lights, getting the sound right, and creating bullet points about what I wanted to share. And then, you could hear me say, "I think I'll wait until tomorrow to do the shoot; it's been a long day." The next day, I spent all day circling around the setup, making excuses about "important" tasks that "hindered" me from doing the video. Four days went like this, and I finally got tired of myself and said, "Just do it." I got ready, went in front of the camera—and I froze! I finally made the first video, and within two days, I created a complete video course—in English! Mind you, I'm Danish, so English is not my first language. The first step is always the hardest.

"I learned that courage was not the absence of fear, but the triumph over it. The brave man is not he who does not feel afraid, but he who conquers that fear."

—Nelson Mandela

Fear

If we don't locate where the fear is coming from, it can be brutal on our confidence. We start up our negative thinking, telling ourselves that it probably wasn't a good idea after all, maybe I'm just not cut out for this, some people are so much better than me, and so on. Then we quit. I don't know what stories you are telling yourself, but you likely do.

After I filmed that first video, I was so proud of myself for finally doing it that I immediately called up my husband and practically screamed at him, "I did it, I did it," and he, always being encouraging, cheering, and enthusiastic, went, "I'm so proud of you, I can't wait to see it, tell me how good it is," and I said, "I don't know if it is good, I don't want to watch it. Isn't it enough that I recorded it?!" He laughed and said he would watch it as soon as he got home. So, he did and then said, "Do you even know how good this is? It's really good!" And I finally watched my own first video, and it was good.

The reason I'm telling you this is that the first step took me a long time, but it gave me confidence, momentum, and excitement to do the following steps. Competence and confidence go hand in hand. The more confident you feel, the easier it is to learn new competencies, and the more competencies you have, the more confident you feel. Don't underestimate yourself.

Find the fear that is holding you back or entirely stopping you from reaching your dreams and goals, and ask yourself if there is anything to be afraid of or if it is just a sign that you are leaving your comfort zone and walking into your growth zone. It is tough at times, but the outcome on the other side really makes it worth the effort.

Outside of fears for our physical health in dangerous situations, there are only three types of fear—loss fear, process fear, and outcome fear—and they are all deeply rooted in how we perceive and react to potential change. These fears can significantly influence our decision-making processes and our ability to pursue personal growth or change.

Each of these fears operates at a psychological level, influencing how we weigh risks and rewards. They can paralyze decision-making, prompt procrastination, or lead to half-hearted efforts in pursuing change. Recognizing and addressing these fears is crucial in personal development, as it enables individuals to make more informed, courageous choices about their lives.

Let's go deeper into each type:

Loss Fear

This type of fear is associated with the potential loss of something valuable when we consider making changes in our lives. It could be the fear of losing security, relationships, comfort, status, or identity. For example, someone might fear losing a stable but unfulfilling job when considering a career shift. The anticipated grief and sense of loss can create a powerful barrier to action, as the known, despite its limitations, often feels safer than the uncertain.

Triggers of Lost Fear:

1. Relationships: When contemplating a significant change, such as moving to a new city or starting a new job, the fear of losing close relationships can be

overwhelming. The thought of leaving behind friends, family, or a romantic partner can make change seem overwhelming.

2. Comfort Zones: Humans are creatures of habit, and our routines provide a sense of stability and predictability. Any disruption to these routines can trigger lost fear, as we worry about losing the comfort and familiarity they provide.

3. Status and Identity: Changes that impact our status or identity, such as changing careers or adopting a new lifestyle, can evoke lost fear. We fear losing the recognition, respect, and self-identity associated with our current status.

Overcoming Lost Fear:

1. Acknowledgment and Acceptance: The first step in overcoming lost fear is acknowledging its presence. Accept that it is a natural reaction to potential change. Reflect on what you are afraid of losing and why it is important to you. Then, turn it 180 degrees and think about what you might actually gain.

2. Evaluate the True Value: Assess the true value of what you fear losing. Sometimes, the fear of loss is based on an exaggerated perception of its importance. Consider whether holding on to these aspects is genuinely beneficial for your long-term growth.

3. Focus on Gains: Shift your focus from what you might lose to what you could gain. Change often brings new opportunities, experiences, and growth that can outweigh the initial loss. Visualize the positive outcomes and how they can enhance your life.

4. Prepare and Plan: Develop a plan to mitigate the loss. For example, if you fear losing relationships, devise ways to maintain connections through regular communication and visits. If it's about routine, create new routines that provide similar comfort.

Process Fear:

This fear centers on the belief that the process of change itself will be too difficult, painful, or demanding. It involves the fear of enduring hardship, discomfort, or failure as one tries to implement changes. This can be particularly daunting when the path forward requires significant effort or when past attempts at change have been met with obstacles or failures. For instance, someone wanting to improve their physical health might dread the initial discomfort of exercising or the discipline required to eat healthy.

Triggers of Process Fear:

1. Uncertainty and Unfamiliarity: The unknown nature of the change process can trigger fear. When we cannot predict the exact path, the mind often fills the gaps with worst-case scenarios.

2. Effort and Sacrifice: Significant usually require substantial effort and sacrifices. The fear of not being able to handle the workload or the sacrifices needed can be a major deterrent.

3. Past Experiences: Previous negative experiences with change can amplify process fear. If past attempts at change were met with hardship or failure, this fear can become deeply ingrained.

Overcoming Process Fear:

1. Break Down the Process: Divide the change process into smaller, manageable steps. This makes the overall change less intimidating and allows you to tackle one aspect at a time, building confidence as you progress.

2. Seek Support and Resources: Don't go through the process alone. Seek support from friends, family, or mentors who can provide guidance, encouragement, and practical help. Additionally, utilize resources such as books, courses, or professional advice to better equip yourself for the journey.

3. Embrace a Growth Mindset: Adopt a mindset that views challenges as opportunities for growth rather than obstacles. Understand that hardship is a natural part of the change process and each challenge overcome is a step towards personal development.

4. Stay Flexible and Adaptable: Accept that the change process may not go exactly as planned. Being flexible and adaptable allows you to navigate unforeseen challenges without becoming overwhelmed by fear.

Outcome Fear

Here, the fear is that even after going through the process of change, the results may not be as expected or worth the effort. This fear is about doubt over the final outcomes—fearing that the "grass might not be greener" after all. It's the anxiety that the time, energy, and resources invested in making a change might not lead to improvement and might even result in new problems or regrets. This type of fear is common in situations where the results are uncertain or where there are no guarantees of success, such as starting a new business or entering a new relationship.

Triggers of Outcome Fear:

1. High Expectations: Setting high expectations for the outcome can trigger fear. The higher the stakes, the greater the fear of not meeting them.

2. Risk of Failure: The possibility of failure is a significant trigger. The thought that all efforts might lead to no tangible reward or, worse, negative consequences can be paralyzing.

3. Judgment from Others: Fear of judgment or criticism from others if the outcome is not as expected can also trigger outcome fear. The perceived external pressure adds to the internal anxiety.

Overcoming Outcome Fear:

1. Set Realistic Goals: Ensure that your goals are realistic and achievable. Break larger goals into smaller milestones that allow for incremental success and reduce the pressure of achieving one monumental result.

2. Focus on the Journey: Shift your focus from the end result to the process itself. Appreciate the learning, growth, and experiences gained along the way, irrespective of the final outcome.

3. Accept Uncertainty: Understand that uncertainty is an inherent part of life. Embrace the possibility of different outcomes and be open to unexpected opportunities that may arise.

4. Build Resilience: Develop resilience by learning from past experiences and failures. Use them as lessons to improve and adapt your approach rather than reasons to fear future outcomes.

5. Self-Compassion: Practice self-compassion by being kind to yourself, especially in the face of unmet expectations. Recognize your efforts and value yourself independent of the outcome.

Conclusion

Fear is a natural response to change, but it need not be a barrier to personal growth. By understanding the nature of lost fear, process fear, and outcome fear, and by employing strategies to overcome them, we can navigate the complexities of change with greater confidence and resilience. Embrace change as an opportunity for growth, and let go of the fears that hold you back. The journey of personal development is as much about the process as it is about the destination, and with the right mindset and tools, you can turn fear into a catalyst for profound and meaningful change.

Reflect on this:

- What fear is holding you back right now?

- How can you reframe those fears to empower yourself to move forward?

- What small step can you take today to begin overcoming your fears?

Embracing Courage

Courage is not the absence of fear, but the willingness to move forward despite it. It's about recognizing that fear is a natural part of the process and choosing to act anyway. Each step you take, no matter how small, builds your confidence and propels you closer to your goals. Remember, the first step is often the hardest, but it is also the most crucial. Embrace your fears, take that step, and watch as your courage transforms your life.

Worksheet at: **majbrit.coach/book-resources**

Community

Community or social support is essential if we want to successfully make changes. Success is a team sport, and no one can do it all by themselves. It is critical for your success that you, in advance, know who will support you and who will be holding you back. You have to be willing to leave some people at the train station if they are not ready to go with you on your journey.

Never listen to anyone who tells you why you can't do it. Instead, find the ones who tells you why you can. Seek out a mentor, a coach, or a group of like-minded people who will challenge you, push you, cheer you on, and want to see you grow and shine. Sometimes that means paying for it, but the benefits far outweigh the investment. Time is the only currency you can never earn back, so be aware—it can cost you a lot more than you think.

It was the first time I was approached about being certified as a coach by Brendon Burchard, and I really wanted to, but I was a single mom of three girls, and I told myself that there was no way I could make that investment. Fast forward a few years, and I'm asked again; this time, I accepted and submitted my application. What changed between the first and the second time? Absolutely nothing apart from my mindset.

I realized the personal value I could get from being certified; it wasn't even on my radar that I could make a career out of it at this point. But I got in the room! In this case, the room was full of people who all wanted the same—to make a better life for themselves and others. The atmosphere was out of this world; there was so much energy, understanding, and support that I didn't need a plane ticket home... I could fly!

The certification was five days, but I made lifelong friends during that time, and I always have this group of amazing, talented, and caring people to reach out to and get inspired by. That's the power of community!

The best part is that you can find these groups and communities everywhere, both online and in your local area. Never in history has it been easier to meet and connect with people that share your interests and passions than it is now.

My point is; you will do yourself a huge favor if you adopt the mindset of "either you pay, or you pay." Whether you want to pay with time or money is up to you, but there is always a price to pay.

Facing Challenges

Starting any journey towards personal growth and success comes with its own set of challenges. These can range from internal fears and doubts to external obstacles and resistance from those around you. It's important to anticipate these challenges so you can prepare for them effectively.

Reflect on what specific challenges you might face. Are you worried about time management, financial constraints, or balancing responsibilities? Do you fear failure, judgment from others, or stepping out of your comfort zone? Identifying these challenges upfront allows you to develop strategies to overcome them.

Dealing with Challenges

Once you've identified potential challenges, the next step is to create a plan to deal with them. This involves both practical strategies and mindset shifts. For instance, if time management is a concern, consider how you can prioritize your tasks, delegate responsibilities, or adjust your schedule. If financial constraints are an issue, look for affordable resources, consider gradual investments, or seek out scholarships and grants.

Mindset is equally important. Cultivate a positive and resilient mindset that embraces challenges as opportunities for growth. Remind yourself of your purpose and stay focused on your long-term goals. Surround yourself with supportive individuals who can provide encouragement and perspective.

Areas Needing Support

It's crucial to recognize the areas where you are most likely to need support. This can include emotional support, practical advice, or professional guidance. For example, you might need emotional support to stay motivated during tough times, practical advice on specific skills or knowledge, or professional guidance to navigate complex challenges.

Be honest with yourself about where you need help and don't hesitate to seek it. Support can come from various sources, including friends, family, mentors, coaches, and online communities. Leverage these resources to build a strong support system.

Embracing the Power of Community

Success is rarely achieved in isolation. Embrace the power of community and social support to fuel your journey. Surround yourself with positive influences who uplift and motivate you. Be open to learning from others and sharing your own experiences. Together, you can achieve far more than you ever could alone.

Reflect on these final questions:

- What specific steps can you take to build your support network?

- How can you contribute to your community and support others in their journeys?

- What actions can you take today to move closer to your goals with the support of your community?

Part 2

4 Simple steps

Chapter 5

All change starts with the ability to be honest with one person... yourself!" Anything is possible when you have a path, a plan, and a desire to take action."

-Dean Graziosi

Step 1

Create Your Vision

In this section, we will begin to set things in motion. You now know some of the most common pitfalls and how to navigate around them. Now, we will start the journey of moving forward and getting you truly connected to your dream, your life, and yourself. It really is a journey, not a quick-fix, so trust the process. I promise you that the outcome is so satisfying that it will be worth all your efforts. Just hang in there and let me help you through. After all, this is what I do, and I have proof that it works and it will for you too, even if you might not believe me right now. It's time to pull up your sleeves and start taking action, so let's go!

What Really Matters

I mentioned a little bit about it earlier. You need to figure out what really matters to you and why. This is an exercise I do all the time with clients and at least once a year for myself to make sure that the path I'm on is still the right one and is aligned with my core values.

Imagine, one year from today, you and I meet up on a beach in Hawaii. The sun is setting, turning the sky into a beautiful, calming orange color. We are sitting on the sand, watching the ocean, listening to the waves and the mild breeze running through the leaves of the palm trees. You are so joyful, balanced, and happy. You can breathe freely and you feel so lightweight that you can almost fly. You tell me it's been the best year of your entire life and you've never thought you could feel this happy. What would have had to happen during that year?

Is it a new business, a new job, a deeper connection with your significant other, more financial freedom, more free time, more self-confidence, more self-love? Sit down in a quiet place and reflect on it and write down everything that comes to mind. Don't overthink it. Then take your list and prioritize what needs to happen first, second, etc. This is your goal list.

Whatever is on your list will have to be something you can act on, so you can't write "Then xx would have to stop being a jerk" or anything else that requires a change from other people. You can never, nor should you, control other people's thinking patterns, behavior, or emotions. You can inspire them to do better by being a good role model for them, or if that doesn't work, remove yourself from their sphere.

Reflect on this:

- For you to say "this is the best year of my life," what would have to happen?

- In your career?

- In your personal life?

- In yourself (how do you feel)?

Goals and Anti-Goals

Now that you have created a list of goals, let's set some anti-goals. These are things, tasks, people, or feelings you don't want in your life anymore.

I know I said earlier that you can't order "don't," but this is slightly different in the sense that you are now aware of what you DO want, and in order for this to happen, you will have to do things differently and remove what doesn't serve you anymore. Most people don't evaluate on a regular basis whether what they're doing is moving them forward or is actually what is holding them back. What served your growth and spirit last year may not be what you need now, but it is very easy to fall into the trap of routine without giving it too much thought. If you have ever felt frustrated about doing something that didn't work and you thought to yourself, "I don't get it, this used to be the answer" or "this is what I always do, and normally it works fine," then you know what I'm talking about. You have simply gotten yourself caught up in a hamster wheel of "used to." This happens to all of us, so don't beat yourself up about it.

Right now, you are here reading this book, and I believe everything happens for a reason. There's a reason you are here right now, and the fact that you've made it this far in the book tells me that you are dedicated and ready for change. You have probably tried every stunt known to man in order to figure it out for yourself before getting to this book and in the end realized that you need a new perspective on things. That is exactly why I put my heart, soul, experiences, failures, and successes into this book.

I've made many mistakes, and I faced obstacles, challenges, and hardships just like everybody else. But if I can save you some time and frustration and get you where you want to be faster, then it served a great purpose. Someone once said, "A stupid man doesn't learn from his mistakes, an intelligent man learns from his mistakes, a wise man learns from other people's mistakes."

Don't get me wrong, we all make mistakes and that is the healthy approach to life. You can't try something new and expect to get it right the first time; it's called learning and growing. And that is why you are here in the first place, so take a moment to throw some imaginary confetti up into the air and celebrate yourself.

Back to the anti-goals...

As mentioned, these are things you don't want in your life. That could be negative self-talk, negative people, tasks you hate doing, feelings of sadness. Whatever comes to mind, write it down and understand that anti-goals are not the direct opposite of goals. They are elements that you recognize as detrimental to your progress and well-being. By identifying them, you can consciously avoid or eliminate these barriers from your life.

Reflect on this:

- *What negative habits or routines are currently holding you back?*

- *Are there any relationships that drain your energy rather than uplift you?*

- *What activities or responsibilities make you feel unhappy or unfulfilled?*

- *How can you start to remove or reduce these negative influences from your life?*

Setting the Stage for Success

Now that you have identified both your goals and anti-goals, you have a clear picture of what you want to achieve and what you need to avoid. This dual approach helps you create a balanced and focused path forward. Remember, this is a journey, and while you might encounter challenges along the way, you how have the tools and insights to navigate through them.

Success is not just about reaching the finish line but also about enjoying the process and growing through it. Embrace the journey, stay committed to your goals, and be vigilant about eliminating what doesn't serve you.

Reflect on these questions:

- How can you stay motivated and focused on your goals?

- What strategies can you use to overcome obstacles that arise?

- Who can support you in staying accountable and motivated?

Worksheet at: **majbrit.coach/book-resources**

Confidence-Competence Loop

I told my daughter not to spend time doing her math homework. Now, why would I encourage her to quit doing what she is supposed to do in college? For higher performance!

She didn't like math and she didn't get it. She would spend hours trying to figure it out, and the only result was her feeling frustrated, sad, and worst of all, she lost her self-confidence. She was telling herself that she was hopeless, stupid, and incompetent. It really hurt me as a mother because I know how many other strengths and competencies she has. She took that one thing she wasn't good at, judged her whole person based on that one thing, and made that her baseline. Her performance in other classes went down as a consequence of her lack of confidence. She talked herself down in all aspects of life. So, I told her to quit math.

I explained to her that nobody is good at everything, so focus on what you are good at and become excellent. By removing the stress about math, she could focus on the classes she was good at and passionate about at a whole new level, and she started shining. She was happier, more confident, and her grades went up in everything except, of course, math. I told her not to worry about it because the other grades would even out the average and that the most important part was that she was excited about college and learning again. The good grades in the other classes made her self-confidence grow, and slowly her math grades went up too. That is called a confidence-competence loop.

It's easier to gain new competencies when you are confident, and it's easier to be confident when you have competencies.

I’m telling you this story so you can see that if you try to be great at everything, you will end up being average at best. Focus on what you love and are passionate about, outsource what has to be done, and get rid of the rest altogether. As in my daughter’s case, what you hate doing, being, or feeling will slow you down in all the other areas as well, so this is far more important than most people think. Now, go create that anti-goal list if you didn’t already. I know you will love it!

Your "Why" Is Your Success

Let's investigate why this particular dream or goal is important to you. Whenever I ask people, and I do that all the time, why their specific dream or goal is important to them, they usually answer on "auto-pilot" that it's because they want more money, more freedom, more intimacy, or whatever the case might be. There's nothing wrong with these answers, but they don't get deep enough into your heart, soul, and purpose to make you push through challenges and hard times; that will come when you are in the process of making changes. Trust me, once you commit—life will test you.

Your true "why" lies deep within you and is connected to emotions you are probably unaware of at this point. It is crucial to get this one right. If you don't, everything else will follow down the wrong road as well. Your "why" is the cornerstone of everything else you will learn in this book. The goal is for you to reach your full potential and then later be able to look back at the current you and think, "I've done some really important work."

I was reading a book by Dean Graziosi called *Millionaire Success Habits*, and here I was introduced to the concept of "Seven Levels Deep." A great exercise that Dean learned from Dan Sullivan and that I'm about to teach you here. The core idea of this exercise is to find your true and deepest "why." To do that, you have to get past your head and into your heart.

We are really good at using the logical part of our brain to find good, solid, sensible reasons to do or not to do something. But if it's not aligned with our true feelings, we set ourselves up for failure. Said in another way, the heart always trumps the head. If you think back, I'm sure you can recall a situation where you made a rational and well-argued decision only to find that it didn't work out in the end. Maybe, at the time, you knew your heart wasn't in it, maybe you didn't, but it doesn't matter because the result came out just the same, and you had to do it differently. So, remember that line "the heart always trumps the head" and listen to your heart every time to avoid that unnecessary detour to your destination.

To fully understand this exercise, I had to go through it myself. It was an emotional eye-opener that caused some tears. It will likely be the same for you. Remember, it is supposed to be emotional. You must get into your deepest values and drivers buried inside your heart.

The exercise is simple, challenging, and unbelievably valuable, so let me take you through it step by step. You might want someone you trust to do this with you; it is hard to ask the tough questions to yourself, mainly because you won't recognize if you are "cheating" and staying in your head.

Take your number one dream or goal previously defined and ask why it is important. Then, based on the answer, you ask, "Why is this important?" And you repeat it seven times. Not six, not nine—seven times!

You will spend the first five times in your head and need two times in your heart to recognize what it's really about for you. If you go above the seven, you will talk your way out of your purpose again, so SEVEN is your number.

I'll give you my example here to give you something to go on, and you will also find the worksheet in the workbook chapter.

Example: Seven Levels Deep

My dream was to create a healthy business to support my family without compromising time with my family or my well-being.

Why is that important? (Number 1)

Because I want my kids to have a present parent and have no worries about how to pay the rent.

Why is that important? (Number 2)

Because I want to show them that anything in life is possible and they don't have to settle for mediocracy.

Why is that important? (Number 3)

Because if they believe that anything is possible, they will not be afraid to take chances, be themselves, and stand up for what they believe.

Why is that important? (Number 4)

Because I want them to have strength and confidence in the fact that they are great human beings regardless of their preferences, I want them to feel supported and cheered on in their pursuit of happiness and the life of their dreams.

Why is that important? (Number 5)

Because I never felt like my parents supported me. Anything less than perfect would be commented with a "that's what happens when you always try to cut corners or maybe if you weren't so lazy, you could have done it".

Why is that important? (Number 6)

Because the lack of acknowledgment, even when I did great, gave me a feeling of never being good enough?

Why is that important? (Number 7)

Because I want to be so excellent at what I do and how I do it that I don't have to rely on the acknowledgement from others in order to feel proud and joyful.

By the seventh level, you have reached a deep and emotionally resonant reason for wanting to start your own business. This reason is connected to your core values and will help you stay motivated and resilient through challenges.

This resume is a short and straight-to-the-point version, but I'm sure it makes some sense to you. If you pay attention, you will notice that it took me five "whys" to get to "me." It was about my kids and what I wanted to do for them. We all know that we are willing to do far more for others than ourselves, which is precisely why this exercise is so powerful. You will get to the root of your drive; you will get to "you."

I struggled with getting my parents to accept and acknowledge my efforts, so I kept trying to do better.

Unfortunately, I never did get it from them, and I still don't. As a child, that is tough, but it got me to where I am today. It gave me resilience and the ability to push myself after everybody else gives up. Is that a strength? Absolutely. However, it can also be a curse because I have pushed myself to the breaking point a couple of times. The learning here is that it is a superpower used strategically, but be aware of the pitfalls. The good news is you have superpowers within you, too, and they likely come from whatever struggles you've been facing. Now it's time to flip that struggle into power; it's time to let go of the past and make room for your new story where you can design your life the way you want it to be. It's time for YOU!

Final Thoughts

Understanding your true "why" is a powerful motivator. It connects your goals to your deepest values and emotions, providing the drive you need to push through obstacles. This exercise may bring up strong emotions, but that's a sign you're on the right track. Your "why" is your anchor and your guiding star.

Take some time to go through this exercise thoughtfully. Write down your responses and reflect on them. This clarity will serve as a solid foundation for all the actions you take moving forward. Your journey towards achieving your dreams and goals starts with understanding why they matter to you.

By connecting deeply with your "why," you will have the emotional fuel to drive your journey towards success. Let's continue this journey with a clear purpose and unwavering commitment to achieving what truly matters to you.

The Story You Tell Yourself

Right now, you might feel some resistance deep down. You know that what you just read is powerful. On a conceptual level, you understand it. Still, your subconscious mind will try to fight it and say things like, "Yeah, well, that's all good for other people, maybe, but not for me. I can't do this." It is, of course, nonsense. Everybody can do it, and you can do it too!

Let me explain a little bit about how the brain works. It's pretty simple; it does what you tell it to do, which means you can tell it to do things differently. There's only one catch here: the brain doesn't like change. So, it takes whatever information you have conditioned it with as truth and acts accordingly.

For example, as children, we need to learn a lot, like walking and riding a bike. We play to develop our physiological skills, and later on, we want to expand our creativity. We build and invent all sorts of things;

think about all the times you did something fun, creative, and innovative as a child. I bet you did. I also bet that you have repeatedly heard, "Be careful, watch out, are you sure, it's not safe, what if xxx, have you thought this through" and so on, and so on...

Those words were most likely said to you out of love and to protect you, but at the same time, they conditioned you to believe that you couldn't, would fail, would get hurt, and shouldn't even try. The same goes for your childhood dreams of being an astronaut, a beauty queen, or whatever your big dream was. Up until the age of 10, it was okay to have big dreams, but then we're told to grow up and get real. My parents told me, "It is time for you to figure out what (not who) you want to be," and I said I already knew I wanted to be a brain surgeon for kids, and my parents would say, "Yeah well, you can't. So, get back to planet Earth and choose something realistic."

So, we are conditioned throughout life to "play it safe" and keep telling ourselves that we can't. Here the brain feels safe and comfortable and protects us from danger.

Changing the Narrative

Take a moment to think about what dream or dreams you have or had that you never pursued and why that is. Once you answer that, you will know the story you have been telling yourself about why you can't. It is time to create a new story about why you CAN.

You can flip the negative beliefs you have into positive beliefs. Change "What if it doesn't work" to "It will work; I believe in my ability to figure things out."

Repetition is the mother of skills, so you must consistently repeat your new story to yourself. Keep telling yourself, "I can," "I will," "I am." Don't get thrown off because it doesn't work the first time because it won't. You have spent years creating your current internal dialogue and must be dedicated and consistent in changing that habit for a new one—a new one where you believe in yourself. So, keep telling yourself why you CAN and repeat it enough for your brain to accept it as the new truth. It is just a habit; you can change it into a positive internal dialogue.

Reflect on these prompts:

- I am great at...

- 1.
- 2.
- 3.

- I can do ________, because I______

- 1.
- 2.
- 3.

- I will commit to ________, because it's important to me for_____ reason...

- 1.
- 2.
- 3.

Start With the End In Mind

Now that we established that you can and will reach your goals and dreams and that you have figured out what they are, it's time to start acting on them, and here's a simple way to get started. You always start with the end in mind, that being your ultimate dream or goal, just like setting the GPS in your car. You punch in a destination, and it gives you direction, letting you know how long it will take, what you need to be aware of, and what obstacles to expect.

The same thing applies when you are designing your life GPS. You put in your destination, your goal, or your dream, and then you will reverse engineer by asking yourself what you need to believe, do, learn, and where you need to get support. The support is crucial; don't take on the responsibility to do everything by yourself; success is a team sport. I don't know any successful people who didn't get support on their journey, and I know many successful people.

Once you have created your map and you know what you need to do and what you need to learn, break it into smaller pieces and repeat. The smaller pieces, the better; it will prevent you from getting overwhelmed. Finally, put all the little bits on a timeline so you always know the next step. We will get into details about how to schedule for productivity later in this book, but for now, have your timeline drafted.

Think about obstacles you might encounter as you go through your timeline. This is not an exercise in discouragement but rather to prepare you in advance for the struggles that will come. Remember—once you commit, life will test you, so you know beforehand how to deal with it better and don't let an obstacle or a minor setback throw you off or worse, make you quit.

Follow the workbook for the exercises, and remember, you and only you can make the changes you want in your life. You are here and reading this book, and that is far beyond what most people will do. You have already taken the first action step, which tells me you have what it takes to create the life you want and deserve, but you have to put your knowledge into action. I'm cheering for you!

Reflect on these prompts:

- I want to change...

- Because...

- So, I can...

- Without having to...

Conclusion

As you embark on this journey, remember that the story you tell yourself shapes your reality. By changing the narrative, starting with the end in mind, and breaking down your goals into manageable steps, you are setting yourself up for success. You have the power to change your life, and this book is here to guide you every step of the way. Keep believing in yourself, stay committed, and take action. The life you want and deserve is within reach.

Chapter 6

Almost everything will work again if you unplug it for a few minutes, including you.

-Anne Lamott

Step 2

Optimizing Your Health

Your overall health consists of your mind, body, and soul. In this chapter, we will look into the areas where you can have some quick wins and lift yourself to a new level that you may never have experienced before or just forgot about. It's time for you to be at the top of your game. To have the time and energy to enjoy dinner, to pamper yourself whether it's by playing golf or taking a long hot bath. It's time for you to feel energized and desirable. It's time for you to go to the storage room and dig out that big bright wall-to-wall smile of yours, the one that makes you bounce when you walk, the one that puts stars in your eyes. It's time for you to SHINE!

Your Energy Is Everything

It all starts with your physical energy. We have all experienced being in a state of fatigue and telling ourselves and others that we are drained, and guess what happens when we do that? We become even more drained. But you need energy to make a positive difference in your life and in the world. Without it, everything becomes a drag; even minor challenges become real hardships.

Think about a time when you could barely get yourself out of bed in the morning and dreaded the mere thought of the day ahead of you. Let me guess, you hated it, and the hate made it worse, and you took a deep dive into a downward spiral. Now, think about a time when you woke up before the alarm clock even went off, and you jumped out of bed excited to start your day. You made everything happen that you set your mind to, you were productive and joyful. You had time to play with the kids, enjoy dinner, laugh, and feel utterly alive.

Can you recognize both feelings? I know you can. You might have to go back a while, but as I describe it, I know you can recall the state of mind you were in during both situations. We have all been there, we have all experienced both scenarios, and I'm pretty sure everyone can agree that the latter is what we want. Before you get all worried about what is coming next, let me calm you down by saying that energy is not all about eating only broccoli and running marathons.

You certainly can if that is your thing, but you can get great energy with less. I know you know how you are supposed to eat, you also know that you need to exercise. Maybe you are eating right and exercising, and maybe you are not, but you know exactly what to do, so I'm not going to spend much time here.

I will, however, encourage you to start in case you know that there is room for improvement. You don't have to turn your life upside down; in fact, you shouldn't. Start with little things that you know you can stick to and then be consistent with that. Once that becomes first a routine, then a habit, and finally a part of your DNA, you can add new things. Don't try to change all your habits at once even though you are all fired up right now. Find a pace at which you can be consistent even when other things in your life challenge you. Enough of the pep talk, you got this! Now let's create that next level of energy together.

The Power of Physiology

Let's take a look at your posture. How do you hold yourself right now as you are reading this book? How do you carry yourself as you enter your workplace? When you pick up your kids? When you sit down to eat? Most people never really think about it, and that results in them having a tendency to shrink their body. What do I mean by that?

The shoulders down and slightly forward, head down, back not straight. This posture makes you look smaller and sad, but not only that; it will keep you in a mentally closed position. Try to sit up straight right now, go ahead, pull your shoulders back, chest out, and smile a huge smile showing teeth and all. It might feel silly, but stick with me.

You see, posture matters. Next time you go for a walk or walk to your office or the supermarket, try it again. Shoulders back, chest out, and smile. A regular one will do, bounce a little with every step you take, and watch what happens. People will move out of your way, and they will smile back at you. You will feel a lot more confident.

Disempowering Emotion

Here’s another exercise for you that was taught to me by Wesley Virgin. There is something called disempowering emotions. Have you ever felt down, sad, upset, angry, resentful, jealous, or just a little pissed off? All of us have. We understand at a conscious level that feeling that way will not be conducive to getting the things that we want. We understand that.

But why do we keep doing it? Because it's familiar, it's a habit for you to feel down, depressed, sad, inadequate, uncertain, unsure. It's not because you are that way; you just feel that way from time to time and to various degrees.

Disempowering emotions are emotions that we want to eliminate. So let me tell you how to stop them quickly and never think about them again. You have to believe while reading this that you can eliminate these emotions of sadness and depression when you feel that nothing is working out in your life. It's essential.

This is how the brain works. It's not because you're a loser. Some of you may say, "Oh, I'm a loser. It just never works out." It's not about that. It's just how you communicate with yourself. What do you do with your body when you feel sad, angry, or depressed?

We know how it feels, but how do you appear with your body language? Your shoulders and head are down, and you talk low and shallowly. "It's not working out for me. I bought all these programs, and I'm still overweight; I'm not making any money, and I have all these kids, and no one's taking care of me or helping me." So, your voice is used as a shadow. It's not that you're depressed. It's not that you're sad, pissed off, or angry. It's because your physiology, your body, and how you move your body will determine your emotions.

Motion creates emotion! What this means is how you move your body will determine how you feel. We're going to change something here. Understand something about sadness. There's nothing wrong with being sad. Sometimes people die, or maybe something you didn't expect happened to you. So, you have a moment of sadness. But to suffer is a choice. You don't have to suffer. And that's what a lot of people do. Suffering is stacking more negative thoughts and emotions about what happened in their life, such as somebody dying. And what people don't realize is that they're stacking these negative emotions because they make it all about themselves. It's not about you, so change the meaning and your physiology.

Practical Exercise

I want you to stand up for a second, okay? I can't see you, but please play along and stand up. I want you to put your shoulders back, put your chest out, and as you do that, I want you to think about something that makes you mad. And at the same time, I want you to put a huge smile on your face with your teeth. Put a big old smile on your face with your shoulders back, chest out, and head up. And I want you to smile hard with crow's feet all over your face. Smile so that your jaws hurt. Smile.

Now, I want you to get mad. Go ahead, but don't move your body. Don't take the smile off your face. I want you to get mad. Do it now. Get mad but keep smiling. Can you do it? Are you laughing right now? How is that possible?

You're supposed to be mad, but all you can do is smile and laugh. Do you know what amazing thing just took place? You just anchored smiling and laughing to the mad moment. And guess what? You can do it about everything.

Your body will anchor in the new feelings, and this is how you disassociate those negative feelings and start to change the meaning of anything in life. Anything you want, that you used to feel negative about, can change by going through this routine.

Final Thoughts

Your overall health and well-being are a result of the interplay between your mind, body, and soul. By focusing on your energy levels, posture, and emotional state, you can elevate yourself to new heights and rediscover the joy and vibrancy of life. Remember, it all starts with small, manageable changes and a commitment to consistency. You have the power to transform your life, and it begins with the way you move, think, and feel. Let's make this journey together, step by step, to a healthier, happier, and more energized you.

The Power of Healthy Routines

All the best performers in the world have routines they religiously stick to; why? Because it is the most effective way to stay in control of your mind, your time, and your day. When you have routines, you follow a plan you designed. In another way, routines exist to ensure your starting point always has a base in moving you forward. In this section, we are talking about optimizing your health. Still, in later chapters, you will find that routines will also come up regarding productivity.

Suppose you don't build a set of routines to benefit your progress. In that case, it is far too easy, and very likely, to fall prey to other people's agenda, and you will be left behind feeling overloaded, stressed out, feeling like you're not enough, that you don't have time or energy to do all the things that you want to or feel like you have to.

Optimizing Your Morning Routine

Every day starts in the morning, so let's look at most people's mornings. The alarm goes off, and they hit the snooze repeatedly until they can't postpone it anymore. They get out of bed and make a cup of coffee. They sit down, scrolling through the news or social media. Most lose track of time, and suddenly they are in a hurry to get in the shower, get the kids up, dressed, and fed, make lunches, eat breakfast, and do whatever else they do in the morning before leaving the house for work. Mornings like this are stressful.

I don't know you, and maybe your morning is entirely different. Still, if you can recognize some or all of the descriptions above, there is an easy win for you right here regarding changing some existing routines for new and better ones.

The Snooze Button

Let's take it from the top. What happens when you snooze your alarm? The so good because you activate the reward center in the brain, but it is terrible for your health and your energy. The sleep you get between every snooze has no real value since you don't have time to go through a sleep cycle.

It takes longer for you to feel awake, and the drowsiness can stay with you for hours afterward. The snooze button can either be a bad habit or an indicator that you don't get enough sleep. The best way to change this habit is to place your alarm so far away from the bed that you have to get up to turn it off. If you still feel tired after you get out of bed, consider going to bed earlier.

Importance of Sleep

There are three critical components to physical health: sleep, exercise, and diet, with sleep being the most important. Ideally, you should sleep 7.5 hours per night between 10.00 pm and 6.00 am. Unfortunately, this is where most people compromise.

However, there are significant consequences of not getting enough sleep. The most obvious is a lack of energy, but it reaches far beyond that. It will influence your mood, problem-solving ability, cognitive skills, productivity, influence, and interactions with others. I could write an entire book on this topic alone, but you get the picture. If you want to take your life or career to the next level, SLEEP IS NON-NEGOTIABLE!

We have all had days when we slept like babies and woke up full of energy and in a great mood, feeling like nothing could go wrong. We were productive, positive, present, and engaging. I know you know what I'm talking about. The question here is, does this image describe 80% or more of your days? If not, now is the time to make some changes.

Hydration

Now that you are out of bed, let's get you fired up for a great day today. When first getting out of bed, you are dehydrated; remember you just spent 7.5 hours in the desert. Drink one liter of water within the first hour of waking up, ensuring a sustained energy level throughout the day. The bonus is it will keep you from getting sugar cravings in the afternoon, and you won't feel drowsy or tired around 3 pm. There's no excuse for not doing this; it's free, doesn't take up time, and works magic.

The First Hour: 20/20/20 Mode

The first hour after waking up, you should focus on yourself, your day, and your mindset. That means no distractions and no digital devices. Don't scroll through the news, don't go to any social media, and don't check emails. When you do that, you start your morning reacting to the agenda of the world. More likely than not, most of it creates a negative state of mind since news and emails are often bad news or problems, and social media can leave you feeling like you don't measure up.

Instead, spend the first hour in 20/20/20 mode. Personally, I have a longer morning routine that I will share with you, but you can go a long way by just implementing 3X20. This means that you spend 20 minutes exercising. It could be some burpees, squats, push-ups, yoga, a walk, or some stretching to open up your body. The point is to wake up and open up your body, not to prepare you for an Ironman. For me, the morning exercise is a 30-minute yoga and stretch.

Then spend 20 minutes meditating or reading something that motivates you. I do 30 minutes of meditation focusing on conscious breathing. I'm always reading books that I find inspiring, educational, and motivating, and that's what I read in the morning for an additional 30 minutes. For you, it can be ten minutes of meditation/breathing and ten minutes of reading. Ten minutes might not seem like a lot, but it's enough to get you started in a positive way, and it's allowed to pick up the book again later in the day.

Planning Your Day

Use the last 20 minutes to plan your day in advance. The purpose of this is to prevent you from having to make up the agenda as you go. Remember, the brain is lazy. If you don't have a plan or a strategy and someone comes along and wants a favor, the brain will find it much easier to follow that direction than to figure out something on its own. If you go through your day in the morning, you can prioritize what needs to be done no matter what and what action you need to take to move any given project forward.

By going through the day's tasks, your brain will start thinking about solutions to the different tasks. You can think about what challenges you might run into and mentally deal with them in advance. All these parts will help you do what you set out to do in a balanced way, keep you on track throughout the day, and save you a ton of time because you won't have to spend time figuring out what to do next over and over.

If you commit to spending time with these few routines in the morning, I guarantee that your day will be far more productive, balanced, and joyful.

Worksheet at: **majbrit.coach/book-resources**.

Final Thoughts

Establishing a solid morning routine is one of the most impactful changes you can make to improve your overall health and productivity. By optimizing your sleep, hydration, and morning activities, you set a positive tone for the rest of the day. Remember, the key is consistency. Start small, build gradually, and watch how these routines transform your life. Let's continue this journey together, step by step, towards a healthier, happier, and more productive you.

The Big Fight

Within each of us lies a hero and a demon, and the one we nurture will become the most powerful. Your demon is the voice that tells you why you can't do something, why you're not good enough, or that you're too old, too young, or too inexperienced. Every time you engage in negative self-talk or dwell on guilt and regrets, that's your demon speaking.

Unfortunately, the demon often dominates our thoughts. On average, people have about 70,000 thoughts per day, with approximately 80% of these being negative. Most of these thoughts are repetitive, making us adept at negative thinking and finding reasons not to pursue our goals and dreams. This negativity isn't inherent; it's a habit formed by our minds. Fortunately, habits can be changed, and we can rewire our brains to be positive and open.

We often talk ourselves out of success using what I call the "worst-case-scenario-in-30-seconds" technique. When we get a new idea, we quickly come up with all the reasons it might fail, make us look foolish, or cause us to lose respect. Even if we decide to proceed, our focus on avoiding failure can attract the very outcomes we fear. Therefore, we must focus on what can go right. We attract what we focus on.

Shifting Your Focus

Our brains are wired to protect us by highlighting potential risks, but this often holds us back. When asked what they want in life, many people struggle to answer specifically. Vague goals like "I want to be successful and happy" are too broad to be actionable. Define success and happiness for yourself. Does success mean living in a mansion and driving a Ferrari, or having a modest home with a loving family? What specific feelings and situations make you happy?

This book, "If You Want Success, Be Happy," is about achieving happiness and prosperity. Start by identifying what will make you happy. Describe your ideal scenario in detail and visualize it as if it's happening now. The imagination is limitless; use it to picture your dreams vividly, incorporating all five senses. Don't worry about how to achieve your dream; focus on the end result. Your subconscious will find ways to make it happen, but it's currently blocked by negative thoughts and beliefs.

In this book, you'll find numerous reasons why you can succeed. You are resourceful, strong, imaginative, and capable. However, we often forget or underestimate these qualities. Focus on the positive aspects of your brain that have been neglected. Whenever a negative thought arises, stop and reframe it. Instead of thinking, "I can't do that because of X," ask yourself, "How can I do this?" or "What will it take for me to achieve this?"

Rewriting Your Internal Dialogue

The brain doesn't understand the word "don't." For example, if you say, "I don't want this crappy job," your brain only hears, "I want this crappy job." Instead, state what you do want: "I want a fulfilling job." This creates a forward-oriented mindset, helping you achieve your desires. By shifting your focus and nurturing your inner hero, you can transform your mindset and achieve the happiness and success you seek.

Solutions or Excuses

Someone once said, "If you want something, you'll find a solution. If not, you'll find an excuse." As you read this, you might smile, thinking of someone who often makes excuses. But do you recognize when you do it yourself? Because we all do.

This tendency often stems from a lack of clarity. We might feel we should lose five kilos, but if it's not important enough, we won't put in the effort. It doesn't bother us enough, and we often say it because we think others expect it of us.

This is where your mental strength comes into play. You need to live and act based on your values, not what you assume others expect from you. We are adept at making assumptions based on societal norms but rarely validate these assumptions by asking others what they truly expect from us.

You've probably done something that didn't feel right because it was expected by your parents, boss, spouse, or friends. The danger is that this can become a habit. Every time you compromise your values, you lose a piece of yourself and move further from your dreams and desires.

The Power of "No"

I'm not suggesting you become selfish and inflexible. Instead, be aware of what others' expectations are costing you. Only one person is responsible for your happiness and success: you. You can't place that responsibility on anyone else. If you don't like where you are, change your situation or get better at saying no.

"The difference between successful people and really successful people is that really successful people say no to almost everything."

-Warren Buffett

If something doesn't feel right, say no. Don't accept things just to be liked or to avoid making others mad or disappointed. Protect your values, boundaries, and self-respect. If you don't, no one else will, and you risk losing your way. We teach others how to treat us based on what we accept from them. Saying no more often gives you greater control over your life.

Taking Action

You might wonder, "How do I do that?" Once you know what you truly want in life, take actions that move you toward that goal. Don't lower your standards to meet the mediocrity of the masses. You are better than that! How do I know? Because you're still reading this book, placing you among the top 2% willing to do the extra work to achieve the life you want and deserve.

Reflect on these prompts:

I want to change...

Because...

So, I can...

Without having to...

Conclusion

Your journey to success and happiness begins with nurturing your inner hero and silencing the demon that tells you why you can't. By defining clear, actionable goals and focusing on what you truly want, you set the stage for positive change. Remember, you have the power to rewrite your internal dialogue, focus on solutions, and take consistent action towards your dreams. You are capable, resourceful, and deserving of the life you envision. Let's continue this journey together, embracing the power within you to create the success and happiness you seek.

Grow Self-confidence

We all get stuck from time to time, and often, our ego gets in the way. When doubt, fear, insecurity, or negative thoughts hit, stop and ask yourself: Is there a valid reason for my thinking, or is my brain just running on autopilot? Your brain is a machine of prediction, basing all thoughts, reactions, and reflections on past information. To change your thinking pattern, you must teach your brain to ask new and better questions and feed it new information.

When I was a new coach, I doubted my inexperience. For my first coaching job, I was hired to coach a COO at a large company. Initially excited, I was soon overwhelmed by doubt. Who was I to coach this individual? I had never held a similar position and knew nothing about the industry. This is a classic example of focusing on the wrong things because coaching is about the coachee, not the coach. My ego took over, and that's where doubt comes from: What if I do it wrong? What if I sound stupid? What if they laugh at me? Doubt often starts with "What if______" followed by a negative statement. This thinking pattern needs breaking, so let's break it down.

As you know, my mission is to help others reach their full potential. If I start doubting myself, it will delay or even stop my progress, preventing me from helping others as much as I want to. We all have doubts, but what matters is reframing them so they don't hold us back. In the case of the COO, my doubt was discouraging and made me feel unworthy, signaling it was a thought worth discarding. I reframed it by creating a new story: "I want to be a world-class coach," instead of questioning if I was good enough to coach above my rank or in unfamiliar industries.

Statements like "I want to" or "I'm going to" are future-oriented and leave no room for doubt. In contrast, "Am I _____ enough?" is a past-focused question that opens the door to self-doubt. Ask yourself if your thoughts are focused on the past or the future.

Growing up, I often felt inadequate, with achievements downplayed by remarks like, "You probably just got lucky." Such comments can drain the excitement from accomplishments. Never let others' lack of ambition stop you. Instead, create an intentional shift in your thought pattern. Ask yourself: What should my new story look like? What are my dreams, wants, and needs? By answering these questions, you begin designing your new story. Your beliefs can lift you to your goals, but only if you know what they are.

Designing Your New Story

For me, it was: I can coach above my rank because coaching is about the coachee. We can discuss any topic and solve any issue together. Again, success is a team sport. If you want to impact the world, start by impacting one person. Designing and living your dream should be fun, not a hassle. The journey counts, not just the destination.

When you have a negative thought, ask yourself: Can you verify it, or is your brain on the doubt carousel? Inner fears rarely reflect reality. Stop basing your thoughts on worries and start observing the world. Many people like you are succeeding at what you want to do. It's possible. You can do it.

Next, ask yourself: Is it within your control? If yes, you can influence it. If not, let it go. We can't control others' opinions of us, but we often assume they think negatively about us without evidence. You have no idea what they think. Their perception is out of your control. But you can control your actions and intentions. Show up as your best self and bring joy—this improves your odds. Decide what you want your new story to be. That is within your control. Let the past and those who want to keep you there be, and design your future and new story. Shout as loud as you can, "I OWN MY DREAM!"

Worry is the ultimate waste of time:

- If you can do something about it, you don't have time to worry.

- If you can't, worrying will not make a difference.

In my opinion, the most limiting belief people have is "I am too/not __________." You can fill in the blank yourself, then discard that thought. This mindset will hold you back and stop you before you even begin. Get in the game—yes, you will be tackled, and yes, you will get dirty, but play the whole game! Don't judge yourself before the game is over and you've given everything you have. It's useful to evaluate, but only afterward. Otherwise, you'll be stopped by your assumptions about what others might think, which makes no sense.

Being a Role Model

Now that you've come this far, ask yourself: What will make me a good role model right now? Do it, even if you are unsure. Continue even if it is difficult. Stand up for what you believe in, sooner rather than later. Help others. Get the education you need now, not seven years from now. Take action on your words and your dreams. When others see you doing this repeatedly, you become a role model of integrity. They'll know your values and say, "You can count on her; she will show up. She always does; she cares." We will always have doubts, but when you manage to continue despite them, you prove you are a role model. That's why the rest of us look up to you.

I don't know you personally, but I am certain I will admire you if we ever meet. You're here, in the fight. You educate yourself, work on yourself, remain curious, and are open to learning new things. You're still on the hunt; you still believe; you've already overcome a lot. That's why you're already a role model by reading this book. Many people could work to develop themselves, but they don't—you do! You already make a difference, even if you don't see it. Look around, and you'll find that people count on you for love, guidance, and support.

Taking the Next Right Step

What is the next right step you can take? Yes, it sucks! What is the next right step? Yes, they cheated! What is the next right step? It didn't work! What is the next right step? Whatever happens, focus on the next right step in relation to your new story. Don't let a situation put your life on a bitter-pause-bitter-pause cycle; suddenly, ten years have passed, and you haven't moved at all. That's where real pain lives. The longer it takes from when the situation happens to the time you take the next right step, the higher the price. Don't let other people or situations rob you of your personal power; they don't deserve to have that power over you. Let them carry their own luggage. Acknowledge that it sucks, but decide what your next step should be. What's good for you and your new story? What can give you joy, courage, and satisfaction? Stop waiting!

Go through these questions repeatedly until you get it right.

Worksheet at: **majbrit.coach/book-resources**

Conclusion

Every moment of doubt and fear presents an opportunity to reframe your thoughts and take control of your destiny. By questioning the validity of your negative thoughts and focusing on actionable steps, you empower yourself to move forward with confidence. Remember, you are in control of your story. Embrace your potential, act with integrity, and never let fear hold you back. The journey to becoming the best version of yourself starts now.

Repetition is the mother of skills.

-Wesley Virgin

Care and connection

Care and connection are fundamental human drives. To experience deep inner joy and satisfaction, these drives must be active. We need to care for others and be cared for by others. However, there's another crucial aspect that many overlook: we must also care for and love ourselves. You might be thinking, "But how can I love myself when I don't love myself?" The key is to stop listening to negative self-talk and start speaking to yourself with kindness and support. This is essential!

You need to treat yourself with the same compassion you offer others. If you're struggling with self-confidence and self-love, there are a few simple steps you can take right now to feel better instantly.

Limit Social Media

Firstly, limit your time on social media to 15 minutes twice a day. If you use it as a work tool, allocate more time but still only twice a day, and start as late as possible. Never begin your day with social media; the first hour after waking up should be completely off-limits.

Why is this important?

When you begin your day on social media, you immerse yourself in other people's worlds. This puts you in a mental reaction mode rather than an action mode. To achieve your dreams, you need to start your day on your own terms, focusing on your life, dreams, and agenda.

Also, what you see on social media is not real life; it's a curated snapshot. The success, the happy family, the joy – these posts don't show the struggles, the conflicts, the challenges of parenting, the messy house, or the piles of laundry. Comparing yourself to these snapshots can make you feel inadequate and like a failure. Or you watch the news and quickly lose faith in all humankind – choose your poison. The mechanisms are the same. Even if you're not consciously aware of it, these comparisons can be stored in your subconscious mind as facts. When you reduce your social media consumption, you'll immediately notice a difference. Your gratitude and joy for your own life will increase, and you'll feel happier.

The Impact of Scrolling

Did you know that, on average, people spend about two hours a day scrolling through social media? This adds up to roughly 1,500 posts daily. It doesn't matter what platform you choose; they are brain-hacking you, and there is absolutely nothing you can do about it. Every single post forces you to do two things: judge and compare.

Judgment: You decide if this is something you want to read, like, or comment on.

Comparison: You compare what you see to your current knowledge, status, or situation.

Imagine doing this 1,500 times every single day. What happens when you re-enter real life? Your brain is primed for judgment and comparison, so that's what you do. How do you think this affects your ability to stay positive and engage with others?

Secondly, constant exposure to social media diminishes your cognitive abilities. It takes more brainpower than you might realize to process the overwhelming information from high-speed content, colors, text, videos, and sounds. This overload affects your decision-making skills, concentration, working memory, ability to understand information, and problem-solving capabilities. Additionally, it reduces your patience and increases self-criticism and criticism of others.

There are far better ways to start your day. Instead of constantly checking social media, set fixed time blocks for it once or twice a day. This practice will help you feel more connected to yourself and others.

Create Me-Time

You need to take care of yourself first! I know you want to be a good person that people like and count on, and I am confident that you are that, but it won't matter much if you burn out and can't be anything for anyone. Let me start by saying: "You are NOT being selfish for wanting to protect yourself, your values, your boundaries, your time, and your sanity!"

I have coached many people who feel like they can't take time out of their schedule to do what makes them feel happy, relaxed, and recharged when so many depend on them. Every time I hear that sentence, I respond that they are, in fact, the ones being selfish by NOT taking care of themselves. I ask them how they think the people they love will react and feel if they suddenly suffer from burnout. They will be sad, feel guilty, and be frustrated standing on the sideline watching someone they love fall apart and being unable to help.

People often expect far less from us than we think; we never ask them and assume we know. We like to be indispensable. I know because I made that mistake, and I will do everything in my power to prevent you from doing the same. You see, when I suffered from burnout, I paid the price by not being able to care for my kids as they deserved. Of course, they got fed and wore clean clothes, but it was all at a bare minimum.

I paid the price of not feeling good enough; I paid the price of failure. But worse, my three little girls paid the highest price; they had to watch their rock crumble, not knowing where else to turn; they suffered from guilt because they thought they were to blame for the whole thing, and you can't tell little children it's not their fault and make them believe it. They paid the price of not daring to come to me, fearing they would worsen things.

So, when we burn out, we are not the ones paying the most significant price; the people we love the most are. That is why it is never selfish to look out for yourself; it's not even a choice; it's an obligation.

Create blocks of time every week for "me-time" and do what makes YOU happy. Let family and friends know that these times are for you only and are non-negotiable. There might be a little confusion, maybe even fuss at first, but as soon as they see the positive effect this has on you, they will love it just as much as you (will learn to). Keep at it even if it feels awkward at first; it can feel stressful because you're not used to having time for yourself.

Still, if you set aside an hour or two twice a week, you will soon find that it will boost your energy and self-confidence. Self-confidence is crucial to success, satisfaction, and happiness in life. When you feel confident in yourself, you don't depend on anyone else for your happiness – you already believe in yourself. You know you can handle anything thrown your way, and when you do, don't forget to celebrate, no matter the size of the win. It matters, trust me.

Celebrate Your Wins

Even the small victories. Nobody ever got the trophy without making a lot of smaller wins along the way. Sometimes it's a win to get out of bed or do the laundry; in that case, you should still celebrate your success. Pat yourself on the back and say, "Well done, you're moving in the right direction." We can't always be fired up and ready to conquer the world, but we still need to feel like we matter and that what we do makes a difference for ourselves or others.

So be kind to yourself, especially on the hard days; that's when you need it the most, and it will give you the momentum to keep moving forward. Your day tomorrow is always a new chance. Finally, accept compliments when someone else gives them to you. They mean it when they say it, so don't undermine yourself by refusing to receive other people's compliments when they give them to you. Instead, say "thank you" and smile.

- Write down three things that need your attention right now, based on what you just read...

- 1.

- 2.

- 3.

- Which one is the most important?

- *What can you do to improve this yourself?*

- *Who can support you?*

Worksheet at: **majbrit.coach/book-resources**

Conclusion

By implementing these strategies, you'll cultivate a healthier relationship with yourself and improve your overall well-being. Remember, self-care and self-love are essential components of a fulfilling life. Prioritize them, and you'll find yourself more capable, confident, and content. Creating time for yourself, limiting social media, and celebrating small wins are simple yet powerful ways to enhance your self-worth and happiness.

Chapter 7

The direction of your focus is the direction your life will move. Let yourself move towards what is good, valuable, strong, and true.

-Ralph Marston

Step 3

Take Back Command

In this chapter, we will go through some tangible actions you can do immediately to spark your new story and actively use the knowledge you have learned previously in this book.

The Circle of Five

The five people you spend the most time with is crucial to successfully reaching your goals, dreams, and visions. Their perception of you will become your self-reflection, meaning if they don't believe you can, neither will you. If they are convinced that you can, so will you be. If people don't support your dream, they are, by definition, your enemy when it comes to successfully reaching your goals. You need to spend most of your time surrounded by those who support, lift, believe in, and cheer you on.

You might not have that at this moment, but you will have to go and find them. You have to be in the room with the right people. Does that mean you should cut off your best friend or your family? Of course not! It means that you need to be mindful about how much time you spend around them if they are dragging you in another direction than you want to go.

You must remember that you are on a journey right now that you started because you wanted something different. Not everyone you would like to share this journey with will have their suitcase packed, and you will have to accept that. You must go anyway; if not, you will sacrifice yourself to fit into their comfort zone. I'm not saying this will be easy at all. They will do everything in their power to keep you where they feel it is comfortable for them.

This is one of the struggles I hear my clients talk about all the time. You will never have friends or family who will give you the truth 100%. They all have feelings, convictions, and assumptions about your role in their life. They have agendas and their own thing that they don't want you to mess with. They have stocks in your life; therefore, they feel like they have something to lose if you tip the balance of your relationship. They won't support you too much because they fear that you will come too far ahead of them, and they won't tell you when you suck because they don't want to piss you off right before game night.

At best, you get about 75% of what they really think. It all comes down to the fact that it is far easier for them to pull you back than for them to step up. At the same time, your enthusiasm might trigger their guilty conscience because they wanted to do something at some point. Still, they never got around to it, or maybe they didn't have the strength to make it important enough, and now you are doing what they didn't.

You are stepping up. You are designing your life the way you want it to be. It reminds them that they failed or didn't take the chance, and it isn't very pleasant to be reminded of that. They will come up with every single reason known to man about why you shouldn't and what could go wrong.

We discussed this previously, and it's not about what you can't do; it's about them and what they didn't do. You must be clear about this because it is powerful when your foundation of people works against you. And you can't blame them; they are just turtles. Turtles that are sitting on a tuft of grass, and the grass is all they can see, and therefore they believe that the world consists of nothing but grass. You are a giraffe; you can see far over the savanna, and you know there is more than just grass in the world. But of course, the turtles won't believe you when they can't see it, so don't blame them. Just don't pay attention when they try to convince you that there's only grass in the world.

You know better and are strong enough to follow your dreams and beliefs. You are reading this book because you want all the tools you can get to make your mission and vision a reality. If you don't have five people in your inner circle right now that can lift and support you, your first job is to go and get them. That can be a local group in your town, a Facebook group, or a group coaching program like mine where you meet other people in the exact same spot you are and who are all fired up and ready to go.

They will support you, cheer you on, always be in your corner, and have no problems telling you when you are doing great and what you can improve. It is a 100% filter-free environment, and it's the kind of environment you need, so go find your peers right now.

Own Your Morning

We touched on this before, but stay with me.

When you first wake up, your brain is in an Alpha state, you are not yet thinking about a lot of stuff, so you are open to suggestions. That's why the affirmations will be more powerful if you do them before you clutter up your brain. Tell yourself, "I'm so grateful NOW that I am powerful/strong/gorgeous/successful/influential/confident," or whatever words you want to associate yourself with. The key is the word NOW; remember, the brain only understands real-time

Your morning dictates your day; if you don't own your morning, you will lose your day. For example, the president of the United States doesn't pick out his clothes in the morning, and with good reason. You might not think you spend much time on that task until you start doing it the night before. Then, you will discover how much time and stress it causes you in the morning. Don't take my word for it; try it for a few days and feel the difference; I promise you will thank me later.

This is just one of many things you can do to take back your morning. We have already been through the 20/20/20 rule previously. In addition, take as many tasks as possible and do them the night before; it can be making the lunches, packing backpacks, the clothes as mentioned, and whatever else you do in the morning that can be done at night instead. This will help you create a more calm and easy start to the day for you and your family; if you have younger kids, it is extremely helpful in avoiding stressful mornings.

Focus Blocks

I have, on average, saved my high-paying 101 clients two hours and 57 minutes per day, every day, just by doing what I am about to teach you here, so pay close attention, okay?!

You have already planned your day in chapter 6, and now it is time to make sure you stick to your plan as much as possible. I get it; life happens, people interrupt, tasks take longer than planned, and your day rarely turns out exactly as planned. Still, without a strategy to at least try to make the most of your time, you can busy yourself out of a quality-life real fast.

We all get distracted, and those distractions are costly, time-wise. Brendon Burchard made a study with 10,000 CEOs from different size companies, different branches, and different countries worldwide because he wanted to know how much time a single interruption/distraction costs in reality.

The average time cost was 57 minutes. The reason for that is that one interruption never stands alone. Let me give you an example. You are sitting at your desk and working on a presentation, and a colleague asks you to help her reach a box of documents on the top shelf in the storage room. You are a good person, so you get up and help. That task in itself takes maybe five minutes, but then, since you left your office, you might as well grab a cup of coffee on your way back.

At the coffee machine, you run into another colleague you haven't spoken to in a while and chat for about 10 minutes. You are now headed back to your office when you figure you might as well get that phone call to your customer out of the way. The customer asks you to send an email confirming what you just discussed. Back in your chair, sending that email.

Finally, you can reengage with your presentation. The issue now is that depending on the complexity of the presentation, your brain needs between 10 and 20 minutes to reach the stage of focus you had before you were interrupted. You have cluttered up your brain with many other thoughts during the past 30-45 minutes, and your brain needs to sort that out first.

This is the exact reason you want to work in focus blocks, meaning blocks of time where you don't get interrupted or distracted but focus on only that one thing. This means that you turn off notifications of all sorts on your phone and on your computer. Even the email pop-up notification, because even though you don't open the email, your brain is already there wondering what it is about, and you will lose momentum. These focus blocks should be no more than 45 minutes long because that is the longest the brain can focus 100%; some have even argued that it's as little as 25 minutes. Set a timer so that when your bud hits the chair, it starts counting down, and when the alarm goes off, you immediately stop and take a break.

Now, it's just a short break, not Netflix and a bag of Doritos. Just two minutes to get up, stretch out, take a couple of deep breaths and fill your water glass. That's it! That's all the rest your eyes and brain need for you to be back at 100%; pretty amazing, right?!

You can create three focus blocks a day where you only focus on ONE task at a time, starting with the most important. In that case, you will find that you get more done in those two hours and 15 minutes than you usually get done in an entire day.

At the end of every day, you should sit and write down the six most important tasks for tomorrow and prioritize them, and that's what goes into your focus blocks. But, again, remember that it's the most important, not the most urgent.

Urgency often comes from other people being unable to manage their own stuff. You can't fix everybody else's train wreck just because you are good at what you do. If you try, you will find that at the end of the day, you have been putting out fires and accomplished nothing of what could move YOU forward, leading to dissatisfaction and a feeling of not doing or being enough. Other people's emergencies are not your problem; their lack of order, productivity, or time management should never stop you from moving your projects forward.

False Deadlines

Watch out for false deadlines. People will present you to them all the time. I bet you have tried getting a task with an insane deadline, so you had to cancel everything on your calendar and skip dinner with the family to make it on time. You then have one question before you can finalize the job, and they take three weeks to get back to you with an answer. This is a very common example, and I see it all the time. It's not that people are jerks; they just seem to forget that they are not the only person you have to serve in the world.

They don't think about it, so it is your job to make them. I was at one point working with a large oil and gas company, and I had more than 50 contacts within that company. We did leak sealing on offshore platforms. Since leaks on an oil and gas platform are hazardous, many of the phone calls I received were emergencies, but not all of them. That didn't mean that the contact didn't perceive it that way; to them, everything was urgent until one day, when I had to choose between cases because we couldn't serve all of them.

So, I asked the guy on the phone, "When is your drop-dead deadline. The deadline where the platform explodes, lives are lost, our reputation is shattered beyond repair, and you and I are without a job – that deadline! He got quiet, and I kept my mouth shut. He finally said, "are you serious?" and I said, "yes, because everything before that deadline is your preference, but I cannot prioritize my time based on you guy's preferences" he then replied, "I never thought about it that way," and that is exactly my point here.

It turned out that what he initially laid out as an emergency he didn't need taken care of until three and a half weeks later. I had to use this with only two of my contacts. Then they spread the word, and ever since, they always said "as soon as possible but no later than the 14th" or whatever the absolute deadline was. Now that makes it possible to plan and prioritize.

I recommend you ask for their drop-dead deadline, and you can use the line above to emphasize that you are serious. You will likely get the same response I did. I have done this with so many people, and never once did anyone get mad at me because they recognized that I could serve everyone better this way, and so will you.

Say NO More Often

We have already talked about the importance of saying "no." Before saying yes to something, ensure the task meets some essential criteria. Is it something I will enjoy? Will it move me forward? Will it make me a good role model? Is the outcome worth the time investment? These are just some of the questions you can ask yourself to avoid saying yes on autopilot out of old habits.

When you say no, make sure it's a clear and non-negotiable no. If you answer, "well, I'd love to help you, but I simply don't have time," then you can be sure they will come back an hour later or a day later and ask you again. This dance will repeat itself until they ask you for the seventh time, and you feel like you can't say no anymore, and you end up saying yes after all. People take it for face value when you say you can't right now, they don't get that you are just trying to let them down nicely, and you will end up annoyed with them, and they don't understand why. You must express yourself explicitly so there is no room for ifs and buts.

Of course, you can't be a mean jerk to people; they come to you because they trust you can make a difference. You can start by telling them you appreciate them for trusting you enough to do this (nurturing their ego), then tell them that. Unfortunately, you don't share their passion for this particular thing, and you think they deserve someone as passionate as them.

This is usually enough, but sometimes you run into a situation with, for instance, the boss that doesn't care if you are passionate about it. In those cases, you need to add an extra element. Your first priority must still be you and your health, balance, and sanity. So, if the boss is too demanding, you can say, "Sure, I can do that. What on my current list do you want me to delete"? Or you can say, "I can't take on this because it will be impossible for me to do it with excellence." The boss can't really say he doesn't care in this situation because you can always say that excellence matters to you, and that is how you work and why he hired you in the first place.

If you really do want to do something but don't have time at the moment, let the person asking you know that if they can wait two days or two weeks or however long it takes before you can honestly commit to it, then you will love to help, if not you understand that they will have to find someone else.

The positive outcome of this way of doing it is that nobody gets offended or mad; how could they when you are, in fact, looking out for their best interest and helping them get a valuable outcome. They are much more likely to get mad at you if you say yes and then don't deliver at the level they expect, and you hardly ever will if you hate the fact that you said yes. So, if you are still having a hard time imagining yourself saying no to others, think about it like this; have enough respect for them to say no so they can find someone who can give them what they deserve. Backward I know, but sometimes that is what resonates the best.

Acknowledge Your Efforts

You do a ton of things every single day that you likely don't acknowledge. It could be some things that have to get done, like laundry, making dinner, grocery shopping, or mowing the lawn. These tasks are all part of making your everyday life run smoothly, but it also takes time. Time you likely don't consider when you think about what you have been doing all day.

Most people reflect on their day in the evening; it could be at the dinner table when your spouse asks about your day. The problem with this general strategy is that most people in this situation will list all the things they should have done and all the issues that cause them not to do it.

We must ask ourselves and others a different question, like “What did you do today”? The fact is that unless you spent the entire day playing G.T.A. or watching kittens on YouTube, you did do a lot, and you need to acknowledge that. You can create a battle board to make this very real to you and those around you.

A battle board is four squares on paper, a whiteboard, or on your wall using painter’s tape and stick-it notes. It doesn’t matter what’s important is that it is NOT on your computer.

On the top left square, write DONE; on the top right square, write PROJECT; on the bottom left, write TASKS; and finally, on the bottom right, write PENDING.

The order of this matters because we read from the top left, which means that the first things you see are the things you have already done. I give you permission to celebrate yourself. That could be a loud “YES”! a pad on your shoulder, a high jump, or whatever puts a big old wall-to-wall smile on your face. How you do it, is entirely up to you as long as you do it.

Write your project and a deadline on the top right; this is a reminder to let you know what this battle board is about. If you have multiple projects, you will want to create a separate board for each. If you don't have a project per se or a deadline, leave it blank or put a nice picture of your dream in.

When you have to fill in the square with the tasks, make sure you are VERY specific and split them as much as possible. If your project is to publish a book, you can't just put in "write book." It is too broad, fluffy, and overwhelming, and you will never start. Instead, split it up and put in a "write chapter 1" note some bullet points to what it is about. Each bullet point now gets its own stick-it note. You get the idea.

The last square is pending. This is a parking space for things you can't finish right now because it depends on someone or something other than you. It could be a response from someone like your editor doing proofreading, and you can't finish your chapter before you have it back. Understand that the pending section can only have up to three tasks at a time, and that is to prevent you from moving your entire task list to pending.

When you start a task, you move the stick-it note to pending; when the job is finished, you physically move it from pending to done. There's great satisfaction in moving the notes from one square to the next, and whenever you move one to "DONE," you should be proud of yourself – and celebrate for a second. This will bring positive momentum to your day several times a day.

By having a battle board, you always know what to do and what to do next. You can follow the "snake" as your progress throughout the day. If you think you haven't done anything that day, look at your "DONE" section, and you will realize that you have done far more than you give yourself credit for. You will save a lot of time not having to figure out what is next, and you will overcome procrastination on the tasks that suck.

There is always something that sucks, and those are typically the things we push to the next day with the excuse that we were too busy to get it done today. A month later, it is still on the list. Say, "That's me," if you recognize this. The issue here is that it weighs us much more than we think. It is constantly in the back of our heads, and talking straight to our not-good-enough villain. You might not realize it until you get it done and feel the extreme relief that it is finally off your list. The greater the feeling of relief is, the more space it took up in your subconscious mind.

This battle board will guarantee you a heightened and sustained level of energy, productivity, and momentum – go for it!

At **www.majbrit.coach/book-resources**, you will find a drawing of the board and a description of how to use it.

Work on Your Strengths

Unfortunately, the learning system in the job, school, and life is set up so that we are supposed to be equally good at everything. If we are not great at something, we are told to put in extra effort; if we dislike it, we are told to pull ourselves together. I get it; there will always be things we have to do even though we don't want to, but in the broader perspective, we should be far more critical about what we devote our time to.

Trying to get good at something that doesn't come naturally to you or something you dislike will take away your time, energy, and excitement from the things you *do* like to do and the things you are good at. And at best, you will end up mediocre in all areas. Of course, this works for some people, but since you are still here, I know you are not one of those people you want more.

Take the example of my daughter from earlier in this book.

Go for excellence. Work on your strengths and your passions and master those to a degree where you are impossible to ignore. You will experience a sense of satisfaction, joy, and energy that will serve you and everyone around you.

Write down three things that needs your attention right now, based on what you just read here in step 3

1.

2.

3.

- *Which one is the most important?*

- *What can you do to better this yourself?*

- *Who can support you?*

Chapter 8

Resilience is a choice. It's choosing to rise above your circumstances, no matter how difficult, and become the person you're meant to be.

– David Goggins

Step 4

Fuel Your Resilience

Resilience is the process and outcome of successfully adapting to difficult or challenging life experiences, primarily through mental, emotional, and behavioral flexibility and adjustment to external and internal demands. This is where things are put to the test because, as earlier mentioned, "once you commit – life will test you."

To stay on track in the future, you need resilience to tackle whatever struggles come your way. And they will come! You will experience setbacks, resistance from your surroundings, and things that don't work out on the first try the way you had planned. As a result, you will lose motivation from time to time. And that is all perfectly natural, and it's an essential part of the learning journey. We all have setbacks and challenges. When you are at level 1, you will have level 1 problems; when you are at level 10, you will have level 10 problems; in other words, they will always be there. The key is how you deal with it and pivot back.

Control Your R.W.I.D.

R.W.I.D. stands for the Relative Weight of Importance and Duration. The concept explains that for any given thought we have in our minds, we assign it a level of importance: should we pay attention to it or not, do we assign emotions to it or not. We focus on it for a given amount of time – duration. The more importance we give a thought and the longer we focus on it with importance, the more real it becomes in our minds and the more our unconscious mind repeats the thought to us. The good news is that we can take control of this process and choose to give empowering thoughts more importance and longer duration.

Take a moment to write down what empowering and positive thoughts you need to give more time and importance.

You Never Fail

You will never fail. Either you succeed, or you learn.

Every trip out of your comfort zone will be uncomfortable, but you must learn to love or at least deal with it if you want to grow and change things.

Remember when you had to learn to ride a bike as a child? I'm old as dust, so back when I had to learn, training wheels were not yet a thing, so my father was holding the bike with a broomstick for balance while I got up. He held it steady as I pushed the pedals, running beside me. He let go when he felt I had the balance, and I fell. We repeated the exercise, and every time I could ride a little longer before I would fall until I finally got the hang of it and could do it all on my own. I bet your experience is very similar to mine. The only difference between then and now is that, as a child, you are not afraid to fall. As adults, we are much more concerned about the outcome and how others will perceive us, and we are worried about getting hurt.

This is an example from my life: He pushed me hard in the back, so I fell, slid across the ice, and landed headfirst into the board. "What in the world are you doing?" I asked him, both angry and shocked. He said, "Did it hurt?" "No," I replied. "I knew that and I had to teach you too that it doesn't hurt when you fall on the ice."

I was 27, and Peter was teaching me how to skate. I'd volunteered at the ice hockey club for years but had never skated in my life. One day I was asked if I would like to play on the women's team, and when I mentioned my non-existent skating skills, the answer was, "it doesn't matter; you learn that quickly." But, as an adult, you're afraid of falling and hurting yourself. I was hopelessly blocked here and couldn't bring myself to take the necessary chances to become a better ice skater. So, Peter, who was a semi-professional on the elite team, was called in.

The first thing he did was get me out on the ice and run as fast as I could while he was by my side supporting me until he, out of nowhere, pushed me into the ice. It was the best he could do because when I learned that it doesn't hurt to fall, I learned the skill of ice skating in a few weeks. I was still much better at getting in the way than actually playing the field, but that paved the way for my success as a keeper.

The moral of this story is that we are not always able to see our potential ourselves, and thus we do not move until someone pushes us. A huge thanks to all Peters in our lives who push so that we can experience what we are actually capable of. Think of a situation in your life where somebody pushed you and made you realize that you are far more capable than you give yourself credit for

However uncomfortable or scary these new changes seem, remember nobody succeeds on their first try, and nobody succeeds alone. Don't be a part of the 98% that quit when it doesn't work out the first time. Tell yourself that it's a learning journey, and it will equip you to kick a** when it counts the most.

Bounce Back

When life throws us unexpected curveballs, it's easy to feel like we're knocked down and struggling to get back up. However, the true mark of resilience is our ability to bounce back from adversity and emerge even stronger than before. When something you find unfair, unreasonable, or annoying happens, be careful how you work it. Say to yourself; didn't like it, disapproved of it, what is the next right action for me to take?

Whenever you get stuck, you want to get moving again as fast as possible, and you want to regain focus as quickly as possible whenever you get sidetracked. If you get stuck, whether practically or mentally, ask for help. There's always someone who already went through what you are going through, and they can help you or get a professional to help you, but don't let your ego block the way to your success. You either pay, or you pay. If you pay for support from a professional, you will, without a doubt, save time and frustration. Alternatively, you can do it yourself and pay with time (and likely frustration). Time is the only asset in the world you can never earn back, so make sure when it comes to choosing the next move that you consider which one of the payments is the best for you.

Set DUMB goals.

DUMB stands for Dream-driven, Uplifting, Method-friendly, Behavior-triggered and take action. This means making a plan and taking concrete steps towards your goals. Whether it's reaching out to a mentor or coach for guidance or taking a small step towards a larger goal, every action you take brings you closer to success and will generate momentum and excitement for you to move not only away from what set you back but rather move toward your new story and your new life.

Never compare yourself to others. You don't know their story, and it is not relevant to yours. Only compare yourself to who you were yesterday and ask yourself if you took the action that moved you forward today. And in the same category, never accept criticism from people you wouldn't ask for advice. Instead, ask for constructive feedback from someone who knows what they are talking about; that is rarely the case with those who criticize. To effectively do that, you need a growth mindset. This means believing that your skills, abilities, and intelligence are not fixed but can be developed over time with effort and persistence. By having a growth mindset, you can shift your focus from past failures and mistakes, and instead, focus on learning from them and improving yourself.

Practice self-compassion, it is vital when bouncing back. Instead of beating yourself up over your mistakes or failures, practice self-compassion by treating yourself with kindness, understanding, and forgiveness. Remember that everyone makes mistakes and experiences setbacks, and that it's okay to ask for help when you need it.

Never accept criticism from people you wouldn't ask for advice.

Steps for Building Resilience

1. Reflect and Reframe: When faced with a setback, take a moment to reflect. Is this a failure or a learning opportunity? How can you reframe this experience to extract valuable lessons?

2. Set Realistic Goals: Instead of overwhelming yourself with large, daunting goals, break them down into smaller, more manageable steps. Celebrate each small victory to build momentum.

3. Seek Support: Surround yourself with positive, supportive people who believe in your dreams. Join groups, find mentors, and build a network of like-minded individuals.

4. Maintain a Positive Outlook: Focus on what you can control and let go of what you can't. Practice gratitude and remind yourself of your strengths and past successes.

5. Develop Healthy Habits: Prioritize sleep, exercise, and nutrition. A healthy body supports a resilient mind.

6. Stay Flexible: Be open to adjusting your plans as needed. Flexibility allows you to adapt to changing circumstances without losing sight of your ultimate goals.

By implementing these strategies, you can build resilience and navigate life's challenges with confidence and grace. Remember, resilience is not about avoiding difficulties but about facing them head-on and emerging stronger on the other side. Embrace the journey, and let your resilience shine.

Exercise: Building Your Resilience

1. Identify a Recent Setback:

- What happened?

- How did it make you feel?

- What did you learn from the experience?

2. Reframe the Experience:

- How can you view this setback as a learning opportunity?

- What positive outcomes can you extract from it?

3. Set a DUMB Goal:

- Define a goal that is Dream-driven, Uplifting, Method-friendly, and Behavior-triggered.

- Outline the steps you will take to achieve this goal.

4. Seek Support:

- Who can you reach out to for guidance and encouragement?

- How will you engage with your support network?

5. Practice Self-Compassion:

- Write down three kind things you can say to yourself when faced with a setback.

- Commit to treating yourself with the same kindness you would offer a friend.

By actively working on these exercises, you will strengthen your resilience and be better prepared to handle whatever life throws your way.

Make Every Day Meaningful

Whatever happens throughout your day, making something meaningful from it will keep you grateful and focused on what's going right for you. We have discussed the power of gratitude and happiness, which is a mindset you must adopt to make the tough days easier to handle. When everything is going great, it is easy to be happy. Still, you are tested on your ability to pivot when you meet resistance and hardship. There is always something to be grateful for. If nothing else, be thankful that you are breathing. Adopt the mindset that you can create something meaningful every day. You need to train this "muscle" in the good times so it is ready to serve you during the hard days.

What makes our days meaningful is when we feel we matter, make a difference, and contribute. This can be implemented strategically in your everyday schedule. At some point, it will become a habit and then, later on, part of your DNA.

Making your day meaningful is an essential aspect of leading a fulfilling life. It can help you stay motivated, engaged, and focused on your goals. An easy way to start is to be present and fully engaged in the moment. When you are mindful, you are more aware of your surroundings, thoughts, and emotions. This can help you stay focused on the present moment and reduce stress and anxiety. You can practice mindfulness through meditation, deep breathing, or simply by focusing on your thoughts and surroundings.

Your phone is a great way to start. Ensure it is out of sight and out of reach when engaging with others. If the phone is in your hand, you signal that the person with you is only important to you until your phone lights up, which will automatically take the depth out of the interaction. I know you don't mean to appear disengaged, but that happens, and you have probably felt it yourself in some situations. Be the one to start a new culture and be present in the moment. It's a rare thing these days, and if you can be a role model for presence, you will be way ahead of most people, and others will want to have deeper and more meaningful connections with you.

Relationships with others can help you feel more fulfilled and happier. You can catch up with friends, family, or colleagues during the day. You can also volunteer, join a group or club, or simply smile and say hello to people you meet or compliment a stranger for whatever nice or positive you notice about them. These small acts of kindness will make you feel more connected to the now and others, making your day more meaningful. The bonus of being kind is that you will get immediate positive feedback, which comes straight from the heart, as people, in general, are not used to being complimented, which will make you smile too. It's a win-win-win (one for them - one for you - one for the world).

Set Intentions for Your Day

The next thing you can do is set intentions for your day. Don't overload your schedule with too many tasks or goals. Instead, focus on a few essential tasks that you can accomplish realistically. Look in the previous chapter or get the worksheet from resources. Setting intentions is just as much about how you choose to show up in the world, how you carry yourself, and how you interact with others.

I used to be the kind of mom who came home from work. As soon as I stepped through the door, the kids came running yelling, “mom, mom, mom” I responded in a tired voice, “calm down, let me get through the door before you attack me.” I watched them lower their heads and say “okaaay” silently. I took away the magic and their enthusiasm. They had been waiting hours to tell me what excited them, and I ruined it. That had to change, so I set an intention. The following day I stayed in my car for a few minutes and settled down; I told myself to show up as an engaging and caring mom. When I was ready, I went in. the kids came as always, “mom, mom, mom” but this time I responded with enthusiasm in my voice, “yeah, yeah, yeah” and they froze in surprise for a second, and then they totally lit up. With happy, excited faces said, “you have time”? I said, “yes, I have time. Tell me everything,” and they did. That was three happy girls, and the entire atmosphere changed and lasted for the rest of the day once I let their excitement rub off on me. Since then, I always take transition time before entering a situation involving other people. It is so simple, yet it is extremely powerful.

Learn Something New

Learning something new is another way of creating meaningfulness. It can help you feel more accomplished and motivated. You can take a class, read a book, or watch a tutorial on a topic you are interested in. Challenge is one of the five forward-moving human drives, and in learning something new, you will activate it. Besides, the challenges we make up on our own are significantly more fun than the ones life throws at us. This can help create a natural balance.

In short, making your day meaningful is about setting intentions, focusing on what matters, and finding joy in the present moment. Practicing mindfulness, setting realistic expectations, connecting with others, taking breaks, learning something new, and practicing gratitude can make your day more fulfilling and rewarding. Remember, a meaningful day does not have to be perfect, but it should leave you feeling satisfied and accomplished.

The Power of Joy

Joy is a powerful emotional state that can transform our lives in numerous ways. If you understand the science behind joy, you can create positive emotions through intentional practices and elevate your physical, emotional, and social well-being. Joy is not just a fleeting emotion but a choice of how you perceive and live your life. It's a lifestyle that will bring joy, meaning, and fulfillment to your everyday.

Joy is proven to have several benefits, like better mental and physical health, a higher level of reported success, and a better quality of life in senior years.

Joy also has a significant impact on mental health. Research has demonstrated that positive emotions can help reduce symptoms of depression and anxiety, increase resilience, and improve overall psychological well-being. Additionally, joy can improve social connections and interpersonal relationships, promoting prosocial behaviors and enhancing social support networks. However, joy is strongly influenced by our connections and interactions. Positive relationships can create feelings of belonging and connection, leading to increased happiness and well-being.

If you follow the steps of gratitude, mindfulness, connection, and presence you just read, you are on a fast track to a happier life.

Exercise: Making Your Day Meaningful

1. Identify Meaningful Activities:

- List three activities that bring you joy and fulfillment.

- Commit to incorporating these activities into your daily routine.

2. Practice Gratitude:

- Write down three things you are grateful for each day.

- Reflect on these positive aspects of your life before going to bed.

3. Set Daily Intentions:

- Write down your intentions for the day each morning.

- Focus on how you want to show up in the world and what you want to accomplish.

4. Connect with Others:

- Reach out to a friend or family member daily.

- Practice active listening and be fully present during your interactions.

By actively working on these exercises, you will create more meaningful moments in your day and cultivate a happier, more fulfilling life.

Be A Role Model

Being a good role model is not about being perfect or flawless. It's about setting a positive example for others to follow and inspiring them to become their best selves. Whether you realize it or not, you have the power to influence those around you, especially children. So why not use that power for good? Here are some tips on how to be a good role model:

Live by Your Values

Your values guide you through life and shape your decisions. We have already talked about your inner integrity, and that applies here. If you want to be a good role model, it's essential to know your values and live by them. Your actions should align with your beliefs, and you should be able to articulate why you make certain choices. When others see that you have a clear sense of purpose, it can inspire them to do the same.

Be Kind and Compassionate

Kindness and compassion go a long way in positively impacting others. When you treat others with respect and empathy, you create a safe and supportive environment. You never know who might be going through a difficult time and could use a little kindness. So be the person who lifts others and makes them feel valued.

Be Dedicated and Pursue Your Passions

Whether it's your career, hobbies, or personal goals, pursue them with dedication and enthusiasm. When you are dedicated and achieve your goals, you show others it's possible to overcome obstacles and succeed. In addition, your passion and drive can inspire others to pursue their own passions and goals.

Practice Self-Care

Taking care of yourself is crucial for physical and mental health. I said it before, but it really is that important. When you prioritize self-care, you show others that taking care of themselves is essential too. Whether it's getting enough sleep, exercising regularly, or taking time for yourself, make sure you're taking care of your own needs to be the best version of yourself.

Be Accountable and Responsible

No one is perfect, and we all make mistakes. How we handle those mistakes is what makes the difference. When you take responsibility for your actions and hold yourself accountable, you show others you're trustworthy and reliable. Besides, people are generally very forgiving as long as you take ownership and apologize where it's needed. It also sets a positive example for others to follow.

Remember, being a good role model is not about being perfect. It's about doing your best and setting a positive example for others. You never know who might look up to you, so make sure your actions align with your values and inspire others to be their best selves. You have the power to make a positive impact on the world around you. So go out there and be the best role model you can be. You got this!

The COI – Cost of Inaction

Wherever you are, I want you to consider your COI – cost of inaction.

This is crucial!

What does it cost you not to change how things are right now? You are reading this book for a reason, and if you could figure it out by yourself, you would already have done it. I get that change is scary, but so are the consequences of not changing. So, what's on the line for you if you continue on the path, you are on right now? Is your marriage at stake, is your job at risk, is your children's future behavior on the line because they copy what you do, or are you about to lose yourself and your sanity?

I'm not trying to discourage you or make you feel bad, but this is important. In my more than ten years of coaching, I have found this question to be the one that creates the most profound reflections

It is so because we are willing to do more for others than we will ever do for ourselves. We are not that important, but they are. And if our behavior and choices have a bad influence on our children or if it downright will hurt them, then we are far more willing to take action. It's like we now can "defend" spending time and money on ourselves.

Questions for Reflection:

1. What are the consequences if I don't take action now?

2. What is the ripple effect of those consequences?

3. On a scale from 1-10 (1= not at all, 10= Crucial) how important is it for me to take action now?

By reflecting on these questions, you can gain clarity on the urgency and necessity of taking action. This will help you overcome inertia and make the changes you need to improve your life and the lives of those around you.

www.majbrit.coach

PART 3

Put It All to Action

Chapter 9

You don't have to be great to start, but you do have to start to be great.

– Zig Ziglar

Take Action

Taking action and implementing your recent learning is necessary to achieve your goals and improve your life. However, it can be easy to fall into common mistakes that slow down your progress. Next, you will find some tips to avoid those mistakes.

Don't Wait for Perfection

One common mistake is waiting for the perfect moment or the perfect plan before taking action. The truth is that there is no perfect plan or moment. The most important thing is to start taking action and adjust as you go. Life is constantly changing, and waiting for everything to be perfect will only delay your progress. Embrace the imperfections and learn from them.

Set Clear and Achievable Goals

Without clear goals, it's easy to lose motivation and get off track. Make sure your goals are dream-driven, uplifting, method-friendly, and behavior-driven. This will help you stay focused and track your progress. When your goals are clear and achievable, they provide a roadmap that guides you and keeps you motivated.

Prioritize Your Tasks

Another mistake is trying to do everything at once. This can lead to overwhelm and make you give up or burn out. Prioritize your tasks and focus on the most important ones first. This will help you stay motivated. Break down your tasks into smaller, manageable steps and tackle them one at a time.

Take Consistent Action

Consistency is key to achieving your goals. Don't wait for motivation to strike or for the perfect moment. Make a plan and take consistent action every day, even if it's just a small step. Over time, these small steps will add up to big results. Remember, progress is made through consistent effort, not sporadic bursts of activity.

Don't Do Everything at Once

Nobody expects you to turn around your whole life in an instant, and neither should you. You must have some patience and trust the process. If you start too many things at once, it will become overwhelming, and you will give up within a week. Choose the most important area of your life and take a first step. Then add as you feel like taking on more and more.

Trust the Process

Nobody ever got in great shape by hitting the gym once, so be patient and consistent. The results will come, although it might not feel like it at first. Remember, you have spent years building your current habits, so give yourself the time needed to change them for the better. Trust that the process will lead to the results you desire.

Baby Steps

Baby steps are okay, but be careful not to stay in infancy. You will have to show up bold and courageous and be willing to step out of your comfort zone if you want real results and to make a difference. Taking small steps is fine, but remember that growth happens outside your comfort zone.

Celebrate Your Wins

You've heard me say it before. Make sure you congratulate yourself even on the small wins because they are all a part of what will ultimately take you to the grand prize – your dream life! Celebrating your achievements, no matter how small, reinforces positive behavior and keeps you motivated.

Get Support

I know that I tell you this in practically every section. That's how important it is! Have a support system to help you stay on track and motivated. This could be a friend, a mentor, or a coach. Surround yourself with people who believe in you and your goals, and who will support and encourage you along the way. Having someone to share your journey with can provide accountability and inspiration.

By implementing these tips, you can avoid common pitfalls and stay on track toward achieving your goals. Remember, progress takes time, and the journey is just as important as the destination. Stay committed, stay focused, and take consistent action toward your dreams.

Chapter 10

Your Next Step

You now possess the knowledge you need to change your life, and the fact that you read through this whole book tells me you are not a quitter, so celebrate yourself for that. You are probably all fired up right now and ready to take on the world, and I want nothing more than to see you succeed. I believe you deserve it and I believe you can do it.

Knowledge, however, presents no value on its own if you don't act on it. You need to implement and take action, but I guarantee you that if you do, your life will change and you will be amazed by the power within you and the positive impact you can have on your own life as well as the people around you.

Time to Act

If you are anything like me, you probably read through the entire book without doing the exercises along the way, thinking you will do them at the end, and that is perfectly fine. Now is that time! So go do the worksheets and find a quiet spot where you can take the time you need to reflect. Don't get overwhelmed by it and don't overthink it. You will not get everything right the first time, and that is exactly how it is supposed to be. Remember, it's a journey, so don't beat yourself up because there's something you feel is hard to figure out.

You have spent years building your current habits and beliefs, so give yourself some time to figure out how to design your new story, your new beliefs, and your new habits.

Supporting Your Journey

I want nothing more than to see you succeed in your journey for a life where you can be at your A-game in your life and career without sacrificing yourself and your happiness. But if you just feel inspired and motivated for a week, I didn't do a good enough job in this book. However, sometimes it's hard to tackle old habits and at the same time implement new ones. Only you know how much help and support you need to get the results you want and only you can decide how fast you want it.

What I can do from here is offer you additional help and support.

To make this happen, book a 15-minute alignment call with me. At this call you can't buy anything; it's merely a powerful opportunity for us to connect, understand your goals, and see if my support can help you achieve the breakthroughs you desire.

This is your chance to gain clarity, direction, and the confidence to move forward. Don't let this moment pass by. Take action now and start the journey to your best life. You deserve to live with joy, energy, and purpose.

Book your free 15-minute NON-sale alignment call now at **www.majbrit.coach**

I can't wait to connect with you and help you unleash your full potential. Your incredible journey starts here.

Be Bold

Whether you chose to be additionally supported or move forward on your own, make sure that you let yourself grow, let your dreams grow, and go create a life of joy, energy, abundance, and meaningfulness. You have what it takes!

To your success,

Majbrit

About The Author

Meet Majbrit Bøttger, an internationally recognized high-performance and productivity coach, speaker, and author with over a decade of experience helping individuals and organizations achieve their full potential.

Majbrit is passionate about empowering others to unlock their hidden talents and achieve success. Drawing on extensive research and real-world experience, Majbrit has developed a unique approach to coaching that combines cutting-edge techniques with a deep understanding of human behavior and psychology.

As a highly sought-after speaker, Majbrit has delivered keynote presentations and workshops at events around the world, inspiring audiences with practical strategies for improving performance, increasing productivity, and achieving personal and professional success.

The book you've just read has already helped thousands of people around the world overcome limiting beliefs, unlock their potential, and achieve their goals.

With a proven track record of success, high energy, and a passion for helping others, Majbrit is the ideal coach and speaker for individuals and organizations looking to achieve lasting results and transform their lives. Whether you're looking to improve your performance, boost your productivity, or achieve your wildest dreams, Majbrit is the perfect choice for anyone looking to take their personal or professional life to the next level.

www.majbrit.coach

Link List

For worksheets go to:

www.majbrit.coach/book-resources

For a 15-minute NON-sales alignment call go to:

https://calendly.com/hpl-support/15-min-motivation-call-with-majbrit-bottger

For exploring private coaching go to:

https://majbrit.coach/high-performance-coaching

For leaving a book review go to:

www.majbrit.coach/book-review

Made in the USA
Middletown, DE
19 November 2024

64954785R00113